From
Not Dorothy

From Kansas, Not Dorothy

Essays and more from the heartland

By Amber Brejcha Fraley

Cover illustration by Lana Taber Grove

www.fromkansasnotdorothy.com

ISBN# 978-0-692-22334-5

This book is dedicated to my family, who've made me who I am, for better and worse. Special thanks to my brother, Clay Brejcha, for letting me use some of his Facebook updates. Also, the reader should know that many of the names of the people mentioned in this book have been changed to protect their identities. The recipes may or may not have been tested. I'll never tell.

Contents

Ad Astra per Aspera

We Kansans like to think of ourselves as salt-of-the-earth people, humble, hardworking and honest, and not the least bit interested in your coastal shenanigans. We don't cotton to ridiculous real estate prices, highfalutin clothing that costs more than a car, and we can be slow to warm to what may first appear to be hippie fads like yoga or gay marriage, until we realize that these things are actually as down-to-earth as we are, and then we embrace them with enthusiasm. Kansas has brought forth solid, no-nonsense Americans like Dwight Eisenhower, Amelia Earhart, Bob Dole and Bill Curtis.

But truth be told, the wide open Kansas prairies, where the wind howls unstopped and lightning crashes to earth wherever it damn well pleases, are also a place where wild wantonness is fostered, aching to break free. After all, Bleeding Kansas was an early battleground in the fight for the rights for African Americans and women, and Kansas is where Carrie Nation busted bars with an axe. In keeping with *that* sort of spirit, Kansas has graced the world with such visionaries and freaks as Dennis Hopper, Melissa Etheridge, Gordon Parks and

3

Buster Keaton, you're very welcome. (I'll let you sort out the freaks from the visionaries, but so me of these are clearly both.)

And Kansas is where my peo ple chose to put down deep roots a few generations ago. My mother's mother's mother was a rancher in Nebraska until her husband died and she moved herself and her child, my Grammy, to the big city of Wichita. There, Grammy's mother became a freelance writer and café owner, and not a Christian, but a spiritualist who attended séances where trumpets floated in midair and the dead rapped on tables to let the living know they were still around.

"I couldn't stand all that crap," Grammy told me once.

My dad's dad's dad was a farmer who fled Czechoslovakia's authoritarian Catholic Church. He boarded a freight ship bound for the U.S., landed at Ellis Island and hopped a train to Central Kansas, seeking nothing more than the freedom to raise a family while practicing the ancient art of bringing forth food from rich soil. (Family legend holds that when he stepped of the train in Ellsworth in 1885, he witnessed a gun duel in progress.) When he settled in America, he never set foot in church again, except for the occasional wedding or funeral. As a result, my Grandpa Charlie, a dyed-in-the-wool Kansas wheat and cattle farmer, was also an atheist until he took his final breath on this planet.

"Well, now that you're at the end, what do you think?" my dad asked him the day before he'd depart this world. "Is there an afterlife?" Dad reports that Grandpa replied with a single word before falling into a coma hours later:

"Dust."

Maybe my colorful roots are where all the trouble started.

Park Shitty

Most people believe that the BTK serial killer, Dennis Rader, who murdered ten people between 1974 and 1991, is from Wichita, Kansas. This is inaccurate.

Dennis Rader and his family lived in a tiny suburb just north of Wichita called Park City. Park City came into being in the 1950s as a community of affordably priced houses built to accommodate military families in the baby boom after World War II. The houses were constructed, one after another, row after row, with identical or similar floor plans.

After my parents' divorce, my mother bought a cute little brick home in Park City where she could afford to raise my brother and me. The year was 1981. The house had a fenced back yard for our dog, a sweet little fire place and three small bedrooms. Mom set to work covering our utilitarian white metal kitchen cabinets with blue and white Contact Paper. She filled the walls of the living room with her pencil drawings of nudes and her original watercolors of flowers and old farm machinery. She commissioned a dump truck to drop a load of soil in the side yard that she landscaped and when the neighbors asked her about her weird hill she patiently explained

6

that it was called a "berm." She made the house arty and different and it was definitely ours.

After moving in and settling down a bit, we had a moment to take a breath and look around, and it was then that Park City began to look like a desperate place. It was a town where newcomers were viewed with suspicion and Wonder Bread white folk with mullets and muscle cars filled the landscape. One of our first nights in our new home someone banged violently on our garage door in the wee hours of the night, waking us and scaring us half to death. Sort of like a gorilla beating its chest in the jungle, letting us know we'd moved into someone else's territory.

Moving from nutty, culture-filled, liberal Lawrence, Kansas, to blue-collar Park City was like being hit by an El Camino. But we adjusted and pretty soon, we were accepted as locals, even though we never felt like we belonged.

My brother and I made friends and did what the other kids did: we walked and rode our bikes all over town and hung out. Back then, Park City had no library and no rec center. What we had was a convenience store with a few quarter-fed video games and an abundance of penny candy. There were a couple of pizza places and a few churches. There was a ditch that ran through town that provided multitudes of little boys with hours of muddy entertainment. There were the Girls and the Boy Scouts and years later, several former Boy Scouts would learn that BTK had been their scout leader.

Depending on what type of family you came from—a "good" family, for instance—you might spend the afternoon gabbing with your friends on the telephone. On the other hand, if you came from the type of family that didn't give much of a

7

shit about you, you might spend the afternoon with your friends smoking the cigarettes someone swiped from his parents, or walk the mile down the road to the TG&Y to shoplift some eyeliner or condoms. When I was growing up, Park City had exactly one park with a small public swimming pool. For many kids, the pool was their babysitter for an entire summer while their parents worked full-time at Boeing or Beechcraft.

There was the afternoon that I was walking home from school—I was in the fifth or sixth grade—and a man driving a beat-up Japanese car pulled over to ask me for directions. As I naively leaned way too close to his car window to decipher his mumbling, I realized he had his engorged penis in his hand. The police came to the house to take my statement, but we never heard from them after that.

The Park City police force was a joke. They were slow to respond to calls for help and notoriously corrupt. "Whatever you do," the locals warned, "don't ever tell the police when you're leaving town." Because, they said, you were likely to find your house relieved of its contents when you returned home.

I received my very first kiss from Park City's biggest junior-high aged thug, and the only reason I let him do it was that I was too afraid not to. He followed me off the school bus one afternoon and swabbed out the inside of my mouth with his fat tongue under the big elm tree in our front yard. Afterward, he very sweetly appointed himself my protector, threatening any would-be harassers at school. I'm not sure why he never asked me to be his girlfriend, except that I think he understood that we were fundamentally different from one another; i.e. that he *would* be spending time in the joint someday while I *would* be going off to college. Years later, an old high school classmate sent me a link to his mug shot, taken at the Hutchinson Correctional Facility, a medium security prison in Hutchinson, Kansas.

Park City wasn't all bad. There was this great funky little fast-food restaurant named Carols with a menu a mile long. They'd make you a double bacon chili cheeseburger with a side of deep-fried zucchini if you wanted, but they could also whip up a smothered sancho and a double chocolate malt or some chili-cheese fries and a root beer float.

As a high-school aged kid, my friends and I banged around Wichita in my best friend's Michael's Buick or my crappy Datsun 210, with our big, shellacked hair, skipping class and hanging out at the mall. On Saturday nights we smoked copious amounts of cigarettes, drank whatever alcohol we could get our hands on, and blasted top-40 music out the car speakers while dragging Douglas, a main thoroughfare through downtown Wichita. We had illicit affairs with each other, making out and screwing just about anyplace: the back of someone's car, a quiet park or a bedroom when parents weren't home.

As I reached the age when I'd be graduating high school, I started to really think about my fellow Park City cronies, taking note of the kids who were smarter than their siblings and their parents, silently hoping that somehow, some way, they'd find their paths to some sort of higher education or creative employment and out of Park City. Happily, many of them did. And the ones who didn't? Well, they know exactly where they're at and they're happy with their hometown. As soon as I graduated from high school, I left Park City to attend school at the University of Kansas in Lawrence. Soon after, my mother and brother moved away from Park City, and I never really looked back.

That changed on February 25, 2005. As I watched the media circus that descended on Park City and Wichita—because it was the Wichita police force, not the Park City police who zeroed in on BTK—the images of BTK's house were all too familiar. Though I didn't know the house specifically, there was no mistaking Park City: those cracker box houses crammed together like rabbit hutches at the county fair. And I knew that my friends and I had probably ridden our bikes past that very house a hundred times or more.

As the media frenzy continued and the anguished family members of Rader's victims poured out their pain and fury for the entire world to experience, I couldn't help but be completely unsurprised that BTK had turned out to be one of Park City's own. A couple of old Park City friends contacted me in the days that followed and we shared a lot of: "Can you believe this shit? How creepy is that? That asshole tried to take my mom's dog and she told him to go to hell." (Because in his later years BTK had become Park City's dog catcher.) My brother also phoned me, haunted by the once-innocent memories of his best friend in the second grade who was BTK's son.

Later, while visiting an old friend, we decided to take a drive through Park City. We marveled at the tiny houses, remembering who lived where, and were even able to pick out the small spot where BTK's house had been. After Dennis Rader's arrest, the community purchased the home and bulldozed it, leaving the lot empty. We marveled that though

10

one of the pizza places and Carol's were gone, Park City was now home to a martial arts studio and a Chinese restaurant.

Checking out Park City's website, I was shocked to find that Park City has city sponsored curbside recycling, something that the environmentalists in liberal Lawrence, where I live now, have been screaming for these past twenty-some odd years. And Park City has grown, adding new businesses and homes, and now has six parks and so can finally live up to its name.

To me and my old P.C. friends, though, it will always affectionately be Park Shitty, where I grew up and lost my innocence, in just about every way a person can.

Park City Jungle Juice

Ingredients:
5 2-liter bottles lemon-lime soft drink, preferably on sale for 99 cents each
2 large cans fruit punch
2 750 ml bottles grain alcohol
2 750 ml bottles grape-flavored Mogen David 20/20 (a.k.a. Mad Dog) wine
2 750 ml bottles orange-flavored Mogen David 20/20 wine
120-pound bag ice

Method:
Pour all ingredients into extra-large, clean, 40-gallon plastic trash can. Stir well and serve liberally in disposable plastic cups. Don't let the cops into the house unless they have a warrant. Don't drink and drive.

Serves 50+.

My Exotic Mom

Before my parents' divorce, my mom was the angry lady in the kitchen who occasionally came out to yell at us or spank me, because my brother was a good, quiet kid who was rarely disciplined, whereas I was defiance personified and so was hit almost daily. During the divorce, my mother spent six months in a dark depression, holed up in my grandparents' spare bedroom for hours at a time. After the divorce had been finalized and we had moved out of my grandparents' house and into our own home, my mother emerged from her gloom like a siren from a cave, losing weight and dyeing her dull brown hair a bright, fiery red. Gloria Gaynor's "I Will Survive" became her personal anthem and she let everyone within earshot know that she had recently escaped the worst marriage in the history of humankind, in which she'd been shackled to a knuckle-dragging, zit-popping, nose-picking, ball-scratching clodhopper.

She was petite and brash and beautiful and she began to date with a vengeance. At her peak she was dating five guys at one time. Five guys. And two of them had the same name. I can't remember anymore if there were two Scotts or two Johns, but I do remember that I was the one who usually answered the telephone and from about nine to twelve years old, it was my job to keep those dudes straight so that they each thought they were the only man courting the dating powerhouse who was Sherry.

Sherry loved to dance. She would come home and regale me with tales of shaking her groove thang into the wee hours of the morning, with men of all ages, income and race. She went out wearing fake leather pants that we'd found on sale at JC Penny's, high heels and flashy tops, and she owned the dance floor at Wichita's Coyote Club from 1981 to 1985.

I took it all in, idolizing her. I admired her beauty, her seemingly iron-clad control over men and her control over her own sexuality, a trait I attempted to emulate in my late teens, though I failed miserably. At first, Mom hired babysitters to watch my brother and me, but eventually, Clay and I convinced her that we didn't need one. Teenaged babysitters often brought friends or boyfriends over and ignored us anyway, and we liked the idea of being able to control what was playing on the television or the stereo.

Still, it was scary being ten or twelve years old at home without a grownup late at night. I would stay up as late as possible until I was falling asleep in front of the television, only to go to bed and lie awake consumed with terror. I would think that I heard the back door open and someone rummaging around our living room, and I would pray that whoever was out there wouldn't come down the hall and stab me to death and strangle my brother, or vice versa. At some point I would fall into a deep sleep, exhausted, to wake up the next shining morning and find that Mom was dead to the world in her room, sleeping off whatever glories she'd experienced the night before.

A couple of times she didn't come home until the following afternoon, but my brother and I were accustomed to getting our own breakfasts so it didn't seem all that alarming. During a time when she was going out frequently, sometimes both Friday and Saturday nights, I once asked her to please stay home a little more. "Don't you dare try to make me feel guilty," she said. "I've been through absolute hell and I deserve this." I believed her completely and never questioned her nocturnal activities again. Except, that is, for the one time that I woke up in the night to hear my mother making the most ungodly yowling noises from behind her closed bedroom door, where she was spending the night with one of her boyfriends. Was he beating her? I was scared to death. Panicked, I banged on the door. "Mom? Mom?!" She went quiet and didn't open the door, so I went back to bed, shaken, not sure if she needed to go to the hospital or just sleep off whatever ailment had struck so suddenly in the night.

Mother began to frequent a hippie bar called Kirby's near Wichita State University where musicians and artists and general subversives still hang out, even today. She made new friends and threw elaborate dinner parties featuring her Szechuan cooking. She filled our little house with fantastic food and interesting people. They laughed, joked, consumed gallons of wine and liquor, and smoked on the back porch, while talking about politics and food and music and drugs, all while my brother and I soaked up the excitement.

Money was never an issue as we didn't have any. We never really wanted for anything important—we always had food, clothes, shoes, coats, etc. But Christmases were generally frugal and there was always this sort of background sense of impending doom, like we were one big car repair bill away from being on the street. Somehow, our artificial Christmas tree had been lost in the shuffle of the divorce, so to avoid the expense of replacing it, Mom came up with this idea of cutting a naked bough out of a deciduous tree, spraying it with metallic silver paint, setting it into a coffee can of plaster of Paris and then trimming it with lights and ornaments. Voilà! Each year we were the only family I knew with a Christmas twig, which my friends either found to be extremely weird, extremely cool or extremely ghetto, but I didn't really care, because I knew in my heart that my family was unique and clever. Today, you can purchase pre-packaged painted, lighted holiday twigs in any craft or box store. Somebody owes my mother some serious royalties.

Several times, my mom threw dinner parties for my friends, and she delighted in the fact that most of them were not very familiar with Chinese food. She'd whip up exotic dishes like—and yes, these were exotic to kids from Park City, Kansas in the early 1980s—dumplings, hot-and-sour soup, various stir fries and egg fu yung, which always ended up with us laughing our heads off and yelling, "Fung you egg!" at each other.

My mom liked my friends and she liked impressing them. One evening when she was to pick up my best guy friend and me from a junior high dance, she showed up with *her* best guy friend—a guy she'd told me she'd definitely be screwing if he weren't 15 years her junior—and they were both clearly drunk.

As we sped down a residential street at 40 miles per hour, hitting a bump and briefly taking flight, my mother's friend decided that my friend Michael and I were so much fun

16

that we should just accompany them back to Kirby's Bar where they'd been killing time before picking us up.

Mother was just clear enough in the head to say, "They can't get in to Kirby's."

"Sure they can!" her guy friend said. "They're cool."

The instant we walked in the bartender pointed to the door, shaking his head. "No way."

My mother is a gifted watercolorist, and in those early days after the divorce, it seemed as though she would let loose her talents on an unsuspecting world like a dynamo, becoming the next Georgia O'Keefe. My brother and I roomed together so she could use the spare bedroom for her studio. On weekends, Mom would honestly try to paint, her favorite painting music, Spyro Gyra, flowing from the small space. But after a few years, the grind of the workweek and taking care of a house and two kids took its toll, beating most of the creativity, energy and light out of her. She was bitterly jealous of Dad, a paid art professor. The idea that the university might have hired him on the basis of his own talent, résumé and merits was, according to her, utterly laughable. She maintained that it was a position he would never have landed had she not functioned as his brains, manners and social liaison, throwing key dinner parties, dropping carefully timed bits of information to the right people, and reminding him to keep his hands away from his crotch in public.

Those early days in Park City were the good days with my mother. As my brother and I approached the age when we'd be graduating high school and moving away from home, Mom's mental state began to deteriorate. I think that the combination

17

of the catch-up of her abusive childhood meeting empty nest syndrome created a second mental breakdown for Mom, one from which she'd never fully recover. She began to go out less and less. She stopped dating completely. She quit throwing dinner parties. She began to weed out her friends, sure that many of them had turned against her. She stayed home from work sick more often and changed jobs more frequently. No matter where she worked, no matter how good the outlook in the beginning, something would always go awry that was never Mother's fault. There would be a woman who was so insanely jealous of Mom's beauty that her sheer viciousness would force Mom to quit. Or a man who was so envious of her intelligence that she was sure he was sneaking into the job place before or after hours to sabotage her work. In her last years in Park City, I was terrified my peers would find out our family often subsisted on food stamps, and at some point, I simply refused to help Mom with the shopping.

These days, my mom and I don't communicate well. Sometimes go weeks at a time without speaking to each other. Once, while reminiscing with an old high school friend of mine, she said, "I always liked your mom. She always seemed so ... exotic. She invited me to one of your dinner parties with all the Chinese food. It was great." And it made me a little nostalgic for the old days, when Mother was my wild, glamorous mom, and she could do no wrong, no matter what.

Chinese Dumplings

Filling Ingredients:
1 pound ground beef or pork
2 leaves Chinese cabbage, finely shredded
2 chopped scallions
1-inch chunk peeled, minced ginger
5 to 6 cloves peeled, minced garlic
2 to 3 tablespoons red wine
2 to 3 tablespoons soy sauce

Wrapper Ingredients:
1 package square or oval won ton wrappers
corn starch
water

Plus:
Enough cooking oil to cover the bottom of an electric frying pan
in about ½ inch of oil. Vegetable or peanut oil works best

Dumpling dipping sauce:
soy sauce
rice wine vinegar or plain white vinegar
sesame oil

Mix all filling ingredients together in a bowl. The resulting
mixture should feel sticky and smell pungently WONDERFUL. If
it's not sticky, add a touch more wine and soy sauce. One
should be able to distinctly smell the soy sauce, wine, garlic and

ginger in the raw mixture. If you can't smell a particular ingredient then add more of it.

It helps to have friends or children to assemble these, as this recipe makes several, about 40 or 50 dumplings. For each person helping to make dumplings, mix up a little bowl of water and cornstarch; about 1/4 cup water to 1 heaping teaspoon corn starch. This is your glue. Place a scant tablespoon of mixture into the center of your won ton. With your finger, spread "glue" on one side of the wonton and fold over, firmly pressing the edges together and pushing any air bubbles out of the dumpling. Try to make sure the won ton is totally sealed with no filling leaking out. (If you're using square won ton wrappers, your dumplings will be a triangle shape; if you're using oval wontons, your dumplings will be a half oval.) Place raw dumplings on a plate lined with waxed paper in a single layer, separating layers of dumplings with more sheets of waxed paper. Cover the raw dumplings with a damp paper towel while you're assembling to keep the wrappers from drying out. When you're finished assembling the dumplings, your fingers will be disgusting. Wash your hands well.

My mom always heated up the oil in an electric frying pan. It's this weird square thing that stands on its own and plugs into the wall. You can still buy them, but I don't think many people know what they are. Heat oil very hot. To 350 degrees if you're using an electric skillet. Place a few dumplings at a time into the oil so that it doesn't cool too much—maybe 8 dumplings at a time. Let them brown on one side then turn them once so they brown on both sides. As you finish frying them, pile them on a plate. At this point your dumplings aren't finished as they still have to be steamed. What my mom always did was to carefully put all the dumplings back into the electric frying pan, then, shielding herself with the lid, she would QUICKLY add exactly one cup of water, clamp the lid on the pan and wait for the noise to die down.* Once the danger of steam burns had passed, we'd take the dumplings out with tongs, placing them on paper towels to drain. Some of the dumplings fall apart, but many don't. Serve with dumpling sauce, made by mixing equal parts soy sauce and vinegar (about a ¼ cup each) and float a few drops of sesame oil on top.

Serves 4 to 8 people, depending on how many dumplings they can scarf down.

* Please be advised that to throw cold water into hot oil is extremely dangerous, bordering on the insane. I take zero responsibility if you actually try this recipe and you end up burning yourself. All I know is I've watched my mother do it many times over the years and she always manages to come out unscathed.

Don't Mess with a Kansan's Meat

My father is a glassblower who taught at the University of Kansas for most of his career. Like most teachers he had summers off, which was nice since my brother Clay and I spent our summers with him and his second wife, Mallory.

There were a few summers when Dad had the honor of teaching at one of a couple of prestigious art schools: the Haystack Mountain School of Crafts located on Deer Isle in Maine, and the Penland School of Crafts located in the mountains of North Carolina. Both schools boast gorgeous campuses in temperate climates in out-of-the-way parts of their respective states, where student artists may focus exclusively on their crafts for two- or three-week sessions, with talented, sometimes world-famous instructors, for intense, all-day classes. Many of the students choose to work on their projects well into the wee hours of the night.

Clay and I quickly fell in love with life at the art schools, where we were free to come and go as we pleased, all day long. Dad was busy teaching classes while Mallory was taking classes, so that left us to wander the campuses, going from studio to studio, making friends with the students and trying out various arts and crafts. The students always particularly loved my cute and quirky brother, who showed far more artistic tendencies

22

than me. The woodworking students would give him scraps of wood to shape while the pottery students always had a spare chunk of clay for him to sculpt. One summer, the blacksmiths at Penland made my brother an honorary smith, and he hung out with that crew for most of the entirety of the session. Of course, our faces were always quite familiar in the glass class, as we'd spend a fair amount of time hanging out in the "hot shop," which is glassblower speak for the glass studio.

One of the best features of both schools are cozy, conversation-inducing cafeterias with wonderful food, where students and instructors partake of all their meals, included as part of the school experience. I don't think that Clay and I ever made it to a single breakfast, but we never missed lunch or dinner. We'd sleep in late after hanging out with the students into the wee hours of the night, and on one occasion, when I was about 12, one of Dad's students slipped me some wine. One morning around 2 a.m., we ran into Mallory who was up late finishing a project. She yelled at us to get to bed and we acted as though we were going to our cabin, but we were able to double back in the dark and keep partying.

The food served at both Haystack and Penland in the 1980s and 90s was very similar: most of the proteins are derived from chicken, eggs, yogurt, legumes, and occasionally lamb or fish. They serve lots of salads and local produce. Healthy starches such as brown rice, couscous and potatoes, and lots of clever and bold seasonings round out the menus. Though it's been many years since I've visited, let alone eaten at either school, I'd bet the menus haven't changed much.

One ingredient that was sorely lacking at both schools—for better or worse—was red meat, hence the bold seasonings and progressive recipes, which I suspect were employed to try, for a while at least, to divert your attention from the fact that you aren't consuming any dead cows. But the body cannot be fooled, and make no mistake—for anyone who's familiar with trying to quit an addiction such as smoking or caffeine, the physical sensations of red meat withdrawal are quite similar. Each session would start out the same way: students and faculty would be exceeding pleased with the quality and caliber of the food, which everyone agreed was exemplary. However, after about the second week in the session, someone, often a glass blower or potter, would say with a wily look in his eye, "Don't get me wrong, I'm not complaining about the food—but you know what I really miss? Red meat."

"Yeah!" a woodworker would agree, pushing his fork through that evening's carrot pie. "A big, fat, burger would be really great! A grilled burger with *bacon*."

"Or tacos!" a silversmith would suggest, tugging her hand-woven scarf around her shoulders at the thought of such dangerous pleasures. "Or even better—pork tamales, smothered in spicy chili."

"I want steak," a blood-starved paper maker would declare, her eyes glazing over with wantonness. "A filet mignon with sautéed mushrooms and a glass of Bordeaux."

"Really?" the vegetarian photographer from Boston would always pipe up. "I've been quite happy with the food." Then he'd take a satisfied bite of his carrot pie.

The carrot pie, by the way, is not something I'm making up. In fact, Penland's Carrot Pie Exodus—it was a custard really—occurred during the dinner service of a summer session in the early 1980s. At least half the school, my family included,

24

threw our napkins down in disgust, got up, left our plates on the table and drove to the nearest town for dinner. This was a savory pie, mind you, that nowadays any café could sell for ten bucks with a side salad.

We experienced an even more memorable meal at Haystack in the mid-1980s. One evening, during the dinner announcement made by the school's director, we were charged with a vote. He said that for a special dinner at the end of the session, we could choose to have either grilled hamburgers or a lobster boil, to be held on the rocky shore of the island. Our choice.

Lobster or hamburgers. For any non-Muslim, non-Jewish omnivore, the question was laughable.

Lobster. Or hamburgers.

The vote was a clear majority. Rather than raise our hands like civilized human beings, a blood thirsty cry of "MEAT!" thundered from the guts of the artists as a single voice, leaving a few disgruntled lobster lovers to grumble to themselves and the vegetarians to be reaffirmed of the superiority of their lifestyle choice.

On the night of the cookout, people gathered early on the shore, giddy with the promise of grilled flesh. "I don't think I've ever been so excited over a hamburger!" One of the glassblowers said, rubbing his hands together.

Haystack's head cook came down to the shore. He carefully built a ring of uniform stones on the boulders, filled the ring with firewood then placed a grate over the top. He left to go back to the school's kitchen for more equipment and the precious hamburger patties.

My father eyed the setup with worry. "That grate is going to be too low over the fire," he said.

Mallory also looked over the situation. "You think that's too low?" she asked, her arms crossed.

"Hell yes, it's too low," my father said. "He's gonna burn those burgers if he leaves it like that."

"What do we do?" the Stepmonster asked. Her voice was getting that don't-fuck-with-me tone that it sometimes got.

"I don't know …" my father said, unsure.

Mallory leapt into action. "He's not going to burn up *my* burger," she declared. She bent down and began rearranging the stones. My father, not wanting to contradict her, knelt down to help.

The cook caught them both red-handed. He dropped the case of hamburger patties and asked what was going on.

My father and Stepmonster stood up to explain their position, informing the cook that he was in danger of ruining a whole lot of peoples' good time. The chef would not see their point of view. An uncomfortable verbal altercation ensued.

"We're Kansans," said Mallory. "We know how to cook meat!"

"Fine," the cook said. "You know so much? *You* cook the burgers." And he stomped away.

"We will!" Mallory said, triumphant. She bent down to finish remaking the fire ring. Then she and dad built the fire and put the burgers on to cook. When the fire was right, and the first sizzling burgers were done, they made sure that Clay and I were served first, followed by Dad's hot glass students. Mallory began taking and barking orders like a short-order cook. "You there! How do you like your burger? Another well done. How about you? Medium rare. And you? ... We've got one well done, one medium rare and two medium wells. Coming right up!"

Dad and Mallory fed the entire school burgers cooked to order, about sixty people, if I had to guess. Once everyone, including the chef had been fed, Dad and Mallory got to work grilling and serving up seconds for those who wanted them.

The cook apologized, his stomach full of expertly grilled beef. The Stepmonster laughed, also apologizing.

All was forgiven.

As the sun set and the ocean waves crashed against the rocks and people talked and laughed in the cool Maine summer air, someone began to play an acoustic guitar. As the stars began to appear, we all settled in around the glowing fire to surrender to our collective fix, bellies full not of Maine lobster, but pure, landlocked, all-American beef.

Carrot Custard

This recipe is very close to the carrot pie we were served at Penland oh-so-many years ago. Personally, I would add a dash of nutmeg to this.

Ingredients
3 eggs
1 1/2 cups grated uncooked carrots or mashed cooked carrots
3 cups milk
1 teaspoon salt
3 tablespoons butter

Method: In a large bowl, beat eggs slightly and add remaining ingredients. Pour into greased baking dish, place in pan of hot water and bake at 350°F for about 1 hour or until a knife inserted in center of custard comes out clean. Serve warm.

The original recipe, which I tweaked, claims that one may use turnips in place of carrots. I am skeptical.

Serves 4-6

Cleaning Clay's Apartment

Picasso went through his blue period. My brother went through a disgusting period. He's never been what you'd call a neat person, but he reached the pinnacle of filth in his twenty-second year or thereabouts. This behavior lasted about two years. It was during this time that Clay moved into an apartment to live by himself after a less-than-optimal living experience with three other guys. It was a nice, modern apartment, with new carpet, new appliances, new window dressings, the whole bit. I was happy for him, and he seemed pleased with the place.

The first thing that went amiss was that my brother didn't pick up after himself. This was not unusual, nor surprising. He threw clothes here and there, and left dishes lying around—typical early twenties behavior. But after a couple of months, a positive dirt-image of his body appeared on his bed sheets— kind of like the Shroud of Turin, but without any religious or historical significance. I suspect that the impression appeared so quickly because during this period my brother decided that showering was optional. About the same time, a large, gritty black stain materialized in front of his coffee table. It was roughly the size of a full-grown sleeping Labrador.

"What is that?" I asked. Usually, it's not too difficult to figure out what has caused a stain on a carpet: Kool Aid, motor oil, blood, whatever. This had me completely baffled.

"Oh, that happens when I use one of these half-full cups of pop for an ashtray and then accidentally knock the cup over," he said matter-of-factly. "I bump them off the coffee table every so often."

"Ahh," I said, nodding. Because once he'd explained it, it made perfect sense.

By this time, the coffee table had become a fast-food graveyard. It was littered with several of the half-full paper drink cups containing various concentrations of stale pop and cigarette ashes, orphaned drink cup lids and straws, fast food paper bags that almost always contained the butt-end of a burrito or the last three bites of a hamburger if one was brave enough to look, and several partially eaten packages of Little Debbie pastries.

One thing that my brother and I share in common is that we both appreciate a hot cup of freshly brewed coffee in the morning. But at some point while living in the apartment, Clay ran out of coffee filters. Instead of buying new ones, he kept the last one in the coffee maker and reused it, over and over and over again. Only he didn't empty the filter. He just added a few more coffee grounds to it each day. I wondered why the old grounds didn't mold, but I guess each day the boiling water killed off any mold spores or errant bacteria.

About six months into his stint in the apartment, Clay stopped taking out the trash. Bags of garbage piled up in the kitchen, adding a whole new aromatic layer to the biologic infusion already steeped throughout the place. One day, a cloud of a billion fruit flies exploded from the trash bags, and he did resume taking the trash out after that, after gassing the apartment with insecticide.

But the low point—and yes, there was a lower point—had to be when the electricity went out. It wasn't that my brother couldn't afford to pay his bills, it was just that he didn't want to make the effort. The electricity had been out for several days when I stopped by one afternoon and knocked on Clay's door. He cracked it slightly, peeked out and said, "You don't want to come in."

"Why not?"

"Because I forgot I had a five-pound chub of hamburger in the freezer and it rotted. It smells like there's a dead body in here."

I left.

He removed the offending chub and washed out his freezer. "It was disgusting," he told me later. "The package blew up like a balloon. And believe me, you don't ever want to accidentally poke a hole in gassy chub of spoiled hamburger." I took his word for it. Even though he cleaned up the mess, rotten meat odor has a way of clinging, and the apartment never smelled quite right after that.

I offered to help him clean his apartment a few weeks after the hamburger incident. Clay was appreciative, and we got started the next day. While he picked up around the apartment, I started on the dishes. Every single dish in the apartment was filthy. The dishes not only filled the sink but covered all the counters. Before I could even get started I had to get to the bottom of the pile of dishes in the sink in order to locate the drain. I stuck my hand down into the heart of the mess and came in contact with about two inches of chunky, foul-smelling slime the consistency of snot. I harkened back to my Geology 110 class from a couple of years prior. The snot in the bottom of the sink had a name: slime mold. Slime mold is a living mass made up of single-celled organisms and is one of the oldest living life-forms on the planet. Who says a liberal arts degree is worthless?

I sent the slime mold on its way down the drain, added hot water and soap, and started on the dishes. It took me two solid hours to wash them all. Then I cleaned up the rest of the kitchen, wiping down the counters and the stove. Afterward I collapsed on the couch and assessed the apartment. It looked good. Clay had done a lot of cleaning on the rest of the place while I had tackled the kitchen. The place wasn't perfect—there was still the sleeping Labrador on the floor—but at least it looked and smelled somewhat safe for human habitation. I gazed at the kitchen, admiring my work.

That's when I saw it.

"What the hell is that?" I said.

"What?"

"That!" I pointed.

"You mean the dishwasher?"

A Sampling of My Brother's Facebook Statuses

October 26
Rocks, oxbow lakes, rivers, slideshows, parasympathetic, sympathetic, daydream, empathy, psychosis, the I, the part of, punctuated equalibria, the defensive, calm, at peace, fluid, the static, the transcendental, the formative, the active state, fight or flight, straight rivers, curvy ones, the midbrain, the lateral brain, right brain, left brain...etc.

October 28
(Put on a happy Face: Batman as a schizophrenic savior) Kim Basinger is asked why the film was so popular...her response goes something like how there are three people represented in all of us, and the article hints at how one cannot ultimately preside over another. Makes me think of when I learned in psychology class how the human mind tends to a take to a normative equilibrium. And the Joker say's, "I may be smiling on the outside, but on the inside I'm crying" or some such. Besides...who here is not a fan of *Blade Runner*?

December 13
I have a secret that probably shouldn't get out so don't tell anyone...I have this secret desire to dance to "Waterloo" by ABBA on the Wii console.

Note: The following update will make more sense to the reader who is A) familiar with the appearance of cartoon renderings of

Seamonkeys and B) familiar with the shape of the Kansas City Royals' logo.

December 29

Before your time back in 400 A.D. they used to fill up Royals Stadium with water and have naval battles. The spectators decided that the flailing bodies of the claimed victims looked like Seamonkeys. You know because all people did then was dress up in the latest toga fashion, have sex, and read comic books. Hence the name Seamonkey Stadium. Later they decided that the symbol - which at that time was actually the top of a Seamonkeys head, looked much like a crown and so Royals Stadium came to be.

January 9

So I'm sitting there in my bathtub this morning with a fogged up mirror in front of me because I decided it's better to shave in the bathtub than in front of the mirror, with my right foot propped up on the sink as I usually do. I touch the mirror where my right eye would be so I could see my eye but it made a double exactly where my left eye was. And if I changed perspective, only one eye would appear in the middle of my head. So I move my head in relation to the mirror so that my left eye would line up with the touched spot and all I could see was my left eye. The right eye seemed to share the stereo effect with the left, but the left eye wouldn't share. To make the visuals more interesting, condensation made a "tear" effect and I looked like I was crying.

February 4
Nike Pegasus & Adidas NOVA Glide — Looks like you health nuts
are gonna get me back into some nasty running habits. Don't
forget to keep your liver clean. Eat leafy greens, garlic, cabbage,
walnuts, grapefruit, beets, turmeric, "think brown mustard,"
avacado "if you like avocado," and drink your orange juice.
Some will detoxify the liver, while others produce fat eating
enzymes. Oh, and thank goodness they are finally trimming off
the extra side sole on shoes now. "Um, this should have been
done decades ago but whatever."

February 11
Oh rebel and geek friends—don't you know that if you ask me
to divide by zero; I don't know if you want me to join a
resistance, or if your telling me that Einstein's theory of
relativity falls on its face when it comes to singularities and
black holes.

February 17
Dear Dave Mustaine, you have dropped so many rungs that I
have decided to take an axe to your ladder. You didn't even
mention Ron Paul ... why not? Steve Harris gets my vote for
president now, assuming he plays in my band.

March 5
So I decide to go out and have breakfast this morning. I sit at my
booth and this older dude says "there he is." Says I punched him
in the eye and that I promised to help pay for his glasses. All the
while I'm thinking, "I've seen this guy before." I say to him, "I'm
sorry sir, but I don't recollect that at all." I said to him, "the last

time I've been in a fight was 11 years ago with a marine." Which by the way is untrue, it was an army dude and not the latest incident either, there has been one since and that was also a long time ago. I continue ... "what happened?" he says, "Hell if I remember; it was four years ago ... something about you thinking I got too close to your vehicle or something, a truck." I say, "Well, I've owned a blue Toyota." "Nah, this was a white Dakota." I say, "Well in that case you've got the wrong guy." He says, "Then there's someone here in town that looks exactly like you." The whole time this conversation goes on his wife has her hands over her face with her elbows on the table. Afterward I realize where I'd seen him from: I had sold him some tools from the garage sale. He was probably drinking during this period and somehow got events in his head shuffled.

March 6
Patricia—I appreciate your support for the right-brain ambiguity comment, as we all should know that nothing in this world is black-and-white. Conversely, the left brain is tripped up when it comes to disproofs, or "seemed disproofs" and considering its inability to stay focused on the whole is riddled constantly with error. "Especially while we live in a world that is so uncertain." The combative nature of the left brain to argue no matter what simply because it wishes to win an argument based solely on the fear that ambiguity reigns supreme, and that we must use the creative side to better fully explain ourselves in an "accepting" manner is spot-on. I myself am wholly right brained and am at odds with this world and have seemed only to adopt its errors. I have been interested in this subject and wanted

from time to time discuss this based on extrapolative examples such as the use of Methylphenidate for starters.

Not to sound like a self-righteous right-brained A-hole either. That would go against Patricia's teachings. Even though her final outcome is completely against my own beliefs, or that she ends up sounding to me like an occultist.

April 12
I DEMAND LATE 70s FASHION NOW!

Peeing Under the Train

When Barbara Walters interviewed Monica Lewinsky in 1999, I remember the talk around the water cooler the next day at work and in the media at large involved a lot of bewildered speculation as to what the little hussy had been thinking. Like most of America, I'd watched the interview too, and I was surprised at how stupid people were about the whole incident, because I was pretty darn sure I knew *exactly* what she'd been thinking. To me, it was obvious that Monica Lewinsky was a relatively intelligent, halfway decent looking, hardworking, chubby girl with low self-esteem who was eager to please and who hailed from a broken home. America is *full* of them. All the "party girls" I went to high school with—myself included—came from broken homes. Just to vindicate myself I Googled Monica and sure enough, her parents were divorced. I could see so much of myself in her when she spoke that to me, she wasn't a mystery in the least. She was an embarrassingly open book. When you're the party girl with low self esteem you *can't* ignore any halfway decent looking guy who shows you even a little attention, and you're sure as hell not going to turn down the chance to give sexual favors to someone famous. Any two-bit rock star or drunk actor makes for some great war stories to share with your fellow party girl friends later. But the leader of the free world? That's like the Holy Grail for girls who hate themselves.

Teenage boys are ruthless when it comes to taking advantage of girls with low self esteem, because they're willing to exploit any weakness for the chance to get laid. When a grown man takes advantage of the chubby girl with low self esteem, that's not only cruel, but pathetic.

By the time I was a senior in high school, I was adrift on a sea of depression and uncertainty. My home life was completely falling apart—Mother was having a sort of slow-motion second breakdown, Dad was going through his second divorce, and this left my younger brother Clay and me to pretty much look after ourselves. The only thing that dulled my emotional pain was to constantly distract myself from reality. Thankfully, I didn't turn to drugs or alcohol (well, maybe a little alcohol) but mostly, I avoided my schoolwork as much as possible and strove to be immersed in a never-ending party. I wasn't partying hard, mind you, just partying stupid.

The discovery a couple years prior that I could garner attention—lots of it—by being the loud party girl who liked to screw was as intoxicating as sex itself. High school had become nothing more than an inconvenience. Though I had deep-seated aspirations to go to college, those aspirations weren't just about earning a degree, though that was important. It was also because I knew university life would be the next, bigger party. More guys, more alcohol, more late nights, more illicit screwing … more of everything that kept me from being grounded in the place that the rest of us call "Earth."

Halfway into my senior year of high school I began skipping my first-hour class to sleep in late, so I flunked it. Most days, I went off campus for lunch and never came back again, so I flunked my last two classes of the day as well. I knew I had plenty of credits to graduate high school and I'd scored high enough on my ACT test to get into my chosen college, so I didn't care. I turned in half my homework, showed up half the time and they still gave me Cs and Ds. A couple of times, I came back to school after lunch drunk, which definitely made the rest of the day more entertaining. I'd slept with a decent section of the junior class of boys at my high school because all the boys in our senior class knew I was an emotional minefield and steered clear of me as though I were radioactive. (I think the junior boys knew it too, but they were more desperate to get laid.)

And yet, I still had some standards, a sliver of self-respect. When my government teacher sneered at me and said I was *never* going to pass his class, I aced his final, making my grade for the class a C, because he'd chosen to score the final as half the total grade for the course. When my 29-year old boyfriend said offhand, "You know, I've never read a book," I knew the relationship was in trouble. "What do you mean, *You've never read a book*?" I said, needing clarification. "You know," he blustered, turning red. "I've never read a *whole* book." When he began to size me up to be his five year old daughter's new mother, I knew that the relationship would need to end soon. When he realized that I was serious about

40

going to college and really did have no intention of becoming his child's stepmother, nanny or anything in between, he announced that he was having sex with someone else but still wanted to keep dating me, just in case it didn't work out. That was when I finally dumped him, because I was *not* going to be anybody's doormat.

The first week when college freshmen are allowed to move into the dorms, but classes haven't started yet, is a week that the University of Kansas calls "Hawk Week," when freshmen are supposed to be orienting themselves to campus and college life. But what ends up happening is that college freshmen, like a pack of animals let free from the zoo, lose their minds and party almost non-stop. I was soooo ready for this. My best friends, Michael and Phoebe, and I partied every single night of Hawk Week, sometimes until morning. Once school started, I wasn't doing as well at my college classes as I promised myself I would. Years of declining study habits had taken their toll, and the new-found freedom was just too enticing. I remember showing up one morning for class only to find they'd taken a test the day before I knew nothing about.

One night after party hopping, we stumbled to a popular park near downtown Lawrence known to the locals as "the train park" because of the old steam engine parked there. We ran into two college boys who, at the time, I thought were somewhat odd, but my friend Phoebe was taken with the cute one. We followed them back to their apartment where Phoebe went off to canoodle with the good looking one, while Michael and I hung out with the other guy. He made the lame move of

41

giving me a backrub, the international signal for "I want to fuck you, but I don't know how to verbalize it." He was intelligent and seemed nice, but was sort of soft-spoken and squishy like a stuffed animal. Even worse, he was an English major.

Upon leaving the apartment, I declared to both my friends that I would not, under any circumstances, be sleeping with the unattractive roommate. Within the week, I was sleeping with the unattractive roommate. Over the following six months he would never admit to me being his girlfriend. He took me out on exactly one date. To a dollar movie.

One afternoon after an all-night party binge, Michael and Phoebe and I picked up some fast food, plenty of liquid to rehydrate after our night of drinking, and headed back to the train park. This was before the city had fenced off the steam engine and park goers could crawl all over, on top of, and even under, the train. We decided to eat our lunch on top of the train.

One inconvenient fact about the train park is that there's no bathroom there, the closest public restroom being at the library, about a block away. In addition to being not big on schoolwork, or homework, or work of any kind at that time, I was also not big on walking, running wasn't even in my vocabulary and I'd given up my bicycle for good as soon as I'd gotten my car, a crappy little Datsun that was like a cracker box on wheels. When we made it to the top of the train, I realized I had to pee. Bad. Walking to the library to use their bathroom was not an option. I thought of driving back to the fast food place to use their bathroom, but that seemed like a lot of unnecessary movement.

Not to worry though. I had my good friends, with their good judgment, to come to my rescue. They convinced me that I could crawl under the train, in the middle of the high afternoon, in broad daylight, in a public park full of people, hide behind one of the large, steel wheels of the train, and pee there.

To even get under the train took a few of minutes of wrangling and squeezing and by the time I made it, I figured I was committed. I pulled down my shorts and proceeded to whiz on the ground, squatting as low as I could to avoid splashing pee on my sandals.

For no obvious reason that I could fathom, I could hear my friends laughing at me, though I was sure I was hidden from view. Feeling my temper flare, I began to yell at them. When I emerged from under the train I found my friends lying flat out on the park lawn under the midday sun, gasping for breath. I yelled at them again, knowing full well that I didn't have a bit of dignity, or reason, or self-respect with which to be taken seriously.

Phoebe and Michael then explained that though I *thought* I had concealed myself, once I pulled down my shorts all that was visible was my lower half. My lily white moon shone from beneath the train for all park goers to see. Had I not yelled out, my friends explained, my presence under the train would have been less noticeable, but by screaming bloody murder, I had created the unlikely vision of a white, disembodied ass hollering "WHAT? WHAT?" from under the train.

"People were riding their bikes past the park, cars were driving by …" Phoebe said.

"Kids were playing Frisbee …" Michael put in.

"And there, in the middle of all of it, was Amber's butt!" Phoebe sputtered, in between fits of laughter.

My first few months or so in college I would here and there tentatively reprise my role as "party girl" from high school, until I realized that it just didn't matter anymore. At college, no one knew who I was. I could reinvent myself in any way I pleased and no one would be the wiser, save for Michael and Phoebs. I made a conscious decision to leave that old persona behind, stopped sleeping with any dork who asked if he could, and began the long process of learning to be happy. That's about the time I met Jim, the guy who'd become my husband. We started to talk about sleeping together after dating for a couple of weeks. "If I do this," I said to him flatly, "you'd *better* call me the next day."

"Why would I not call you?" he asked, and I was happy to note he was genuinely baffled by the question.

I figured out that I felt better about myself when I did well in school and worked hard at my jobs, even the crappy ones. I'm ashamed to admit that while I was coming into my own I was still so self-absorbed that I ignored what was going on in my brother's life while he was still living at home. Years later I asked him about it. He explained that he and Mom had never really ever communicated, and my leaving only emphasized that fact. He said she'd break uncomfortable silences by saying things like, "It's so wonderful that we have this time together," and then go back to watching one of the old black-and-white movies that she'd come to consume like food. Meanwhile, Clay was getting himself to high school, doing his own laundry, making his own meals, and getting into trouble with his friends because Mom didn't pay much attention to what he was doing. "Mom pretty much quit cooking when you left home," he said. "I survived on Ramen noodles and frozen burritos."

As for the peeing under the train episode, it was a perfect storm of all my shortcomings coming together at once: my laziness and lack of self-respect combined with a willingness to do anything for attention. It was one of those incidents that, if not a turning point, at least begins to make one re-evaluate one's life.

Still, it's made for a *fantastic* story at parties.

Hangover Cure

For young folks:

First off, the most important thing you can do is to drink lots of water because you're severely dehydrated, which is why you have a headache. Take ibuprofen for the headache, but not acetaminophen, since you've already done plenty of damage to your liver the night before. Call or text your friends, preferably the ones you got drunk with last night. Plan to meet them for food somewhere. Someplace with booths where you can kind of slump over on the tables or in your seats. Wear your sunglasses. Talk about how fucked up you all were the night before and how awesome it was. (Or "hot," or "sick" or whatever the vernacular is now.) Eat something, especially something with protein in it, because it <u>will</u> make you feel better. If your stomach is queasy, try soup. Starchy food is good for your stomach, but still, have some protein with it to counteract all the sugar you downed the night before. (Alcohol is fermented sugar, genius.) If you think you need some caffeine, sip tea or soda. Coffee is probably too hard on your system.

Continue to drink lots of water throughout the day. Take B vitamins maybe.

For older folks:

See above, but instead of going out with friends find something healthy to eat at home and then go back to bed if you can. Lie there and moan or doze if your kids will let you. If there are no kids around, lie on the couch with the television on low volume. Doesn't matter what it's tuned to. Sports if you like that kind of thing, or a documentary. Silence the ringer on the telephone. Flip through catalogs if you want. Then don't be such a dumbass again for at least six months. A year is better. After all, you aren't a kid anymore.

Adventures in a Titty Bar

I worked in the circulation department of a newspaper for a short time while in college. Some days the hours were long, depending on how many times the press or the mailroom broke down. The people I worked with were very down-to-earth blue-collar types. My supervisor was a randy fellow just a few years my senior named Max. Max was a one-man soap opera. He was caught in a drama with his live-in girlfriend Sarah whom he despised but enjoyed having sex with, and Heidi, a girl at the office with whom he was in love and seeing on the side. After dating for about six months, Max asked Heidi to marry him.

Shortly after breaking the news of their engagement, Max told me about a small snag in his marriage plans. Turns out Max had been married to another woman, Kerri, when they were young. They had been separated for several years and lived in separate states, but they hadn't divorced because they were both Catholic and wanted to stay in the good graces of the church. They'd also never bothered to get an annulment.

When Max finally mustered the courage to tell Sarah that he was breaking up with her and she'd have to move out because he was engaged to another woman, Sarah gleefully informed him that she was pregnant with his baby. So there was Max, fathering his still live-in girlfriend Sarah's child, with a diamond ring on Heidi's finger, and legally married to Kerri. I remember that Max was very tired most of the time. Rounding out Max and my department were a couple of college-aged guys. We were a motley crew.

One evening, after we'd put in about a 10-hour day, the guys decided we should all go out for dinner and drinks at a local Mexican restaurant. A few fishbowl-sized margaritas later, they thought it would be amusing to patronize a "gentleman's club" and they thought it would be even more amusing if I were to accompany them.

Sure, I said. No problem. I'd never been to a titty bar before, but what the hell, I thought. I believe in experiencing as much of life as I can. What could it hurt?

As soon as we walked through the front door of the club, I regretted that I hadn't checked the parking lot for familiar vehicles. But then, why would I? There, sitting at the bar was my father, with an absolutely gorgeous scantily clad young woman sitting on his lap. And the *reason* she was sitting on his lap was that in the very recent past, he'd taken photographs of her for her portfolio. So this public display of affection was her way of tipping Dad in addition to whatever money she'd paid him for his photography work.

"Amber!" Dad said. He smiled and waved. I wanted to die.

"Who is that?" my workmates wanted to know. And I had no choice but to fess up, because unlike any other father who might be embarrassed to come face-to-face with his daughter in a strip club, my dad was tickled pink. "I was just about to leave," he said, "but now that you're here I think I stick around a little while longer."

Oh good.

Then, for some reason known only to Santa Claus and unicorns, Dad introduced me to the exotic dancer. I don't remember her name, and I'm absolutely positive she didn't give a rat's ass who I was, but she smiled at me prettily and waggled her manicured nails in my direction. After removing the eye-candy from his lap, Dad insisted on sitting at a table with us. He stayed about an hour, but I can honestly say I don't remember any details of our conversation as I have permanently blocked the rest of this incident from my consciousness.

Gettin' Hitched

They say a woman daydreams about her wedding from the time she's a little girl. Yeah well, not me. I mean, I always knew I wanted to be married someday, I just never thought about the wedding. Not one tiny bit. So when Jim and I decided to get married (a bit too young) we were both completely clueless as to how weddings should go. Him because he's a dude. Me? I have no excuse except that I think most weddings are fantastically boring and I just don't care. To this day, I'm the asshole out in the pews staring at anyone and everything more interesting than the bride and the groom—the little girl picking her nose, the old man whose chin is getting ever closer to his chest as he nods off, the fly buzzing at the church window—all while trying to remember the words to the Lord's prayer and hoping that the ceremony ends quickly and that the food served at the reception is both tasty and plentiful because I'm *freaking starving*.

"Let's get married in a barn!" I said. "In June!" He was 25. I was 22. I suggested that we get married June 18 because our first date was July 18, but July 18 tends to be unmercifully hot in Kansas and of course there would be no air conditioning in a barn. I suggested the barn because while neither one of us is religious, we are very much Kansans in heart and spirit, and if the Kansas wind decided to whip up or if it decided to rain, a barn would be more sturdy than say, a tent. Were anyone to question our choice of venue I planned to point out that the good lord had been born in a barn, but no one ever challenged it. My husband agreed because he couldn't risk contradicting the woman who was having sex with him. What I neglected to consider is that Kansas is capable of being nearly, if not exactly, as hot in June as it is in July. In fact, Kansas can be hellaciously hot in May, or even April if it wants to.

Not only did we have no idea how to plan a wedding, we had absolutely no money. I knew that asking my frugal father for funds for something as frivolous as a wedding would probably be pointless, and since no one else in either of our families was rolling in the Benjamins, I hit on the idea that we could recruit family to help. If everyone pitched in a little bit, I reasoned, we could get a wedding done on the cheap.

My mother immediately volunteered her silk flower arranging skills. We asked my uncle, a photographer, to take the pictures. My dad offered to pay for my wedding gown and a few cases of champagne. My friend Phoebe helped me make the food for the reception. Jim's sister Linda procured and paid for a guitarist to play music. My cousin offered to pay for our invitations as her wedding present to us. I bought matching fabric for all the bridesmaids and told them that they could make whatever style of dress they wished. We'd contacted one minister in town who we wanted to perform our ceremony, but he was busy that day, so we asked Jim's dad, a Methodist minister to do it.

We asked Jim's sister Nancy, who had a talent for decorating iced sugar cookies, to bake and decorate our wedding cake. Later, Nancy would use photos of our cake and her decorated cookies to get a job managing a bakery. At the time, we didn't understand the enormity of what we were asking Nancy to do for us. Honestly, had she just made sheet cakes for the wedding we would've been happy. But Nancy was bound and determined to make us a cake that looked as though it came from a professional bakery. Four months ahead of the wedding she began practicing making icing roses, freezing the ones that came out to her satisfaction. In the end, she used 15 boxes of white cake mix to create a beautiful three-tiered cake. Later she told us she spent the entire wedding day hoping to not soil herself because of cake-performance-anxiety.

I was a little unsure about how to go about finding a barn in which to get married. Then someone clued me in on the concept of "party barns" in our area. In the 1980s and 1990s a few farmers decided to make a little extra cash by renting out their barns for parties, usually the drunken affairs of fraternities and sororities who needed to celebrate away from their houses on campus in order to retain their charters. Nowadays, many family farms are opening their doors to function as quaint celebration venues. But in 1994 when I spoke with the farmwife over the phone, she was audibly surprised. "Oh," she said. "You want to hold the wedding here? We've had a few receptions, but never a wedding."We drove out to the barn to check it out ahead of time, and fell in love with it. The barn was handsome and clean-white with a windmill next to it. The yard was trimmed and neat and the farmhouse was charming. There was a field of brome just yards away, a luxurious carpet of green waving in the breeze.

It was perfect.

When it came to whom to invite, I wasn't sure how to handle my coworkers. Adults who deliver newspapers are a unique bunch. There were several people who threw papers as their second or third job. Like me, there were a couple of other college kids who worked paper-throwing into their school schedules. There was one family who worked together to mow lawns and throw newspapers to make a living. Frank, a delivery driver I really enjoyed having conversations with, was funny and genius-level smart but hadn't shaved nor bathed in years, though the old timers told me that he'd done both when he'd started years before. Things went downhill from there. Frank eked out a living throwing several papers and was my one intellectual buddy out on the docks at the newspaper. We often discussed whatever scientific discovery was currently in the news. When I told Frank I was getting married, he was clearly disappointed. "What'll you do after you get married?" he asked. "Go home and be Mrs. Fraley?" One of the deliverers was a hippie mom who liked the job because she could take her two young kids with her in the car while she worked. One was a wealthy business owner who had a paper route just so he could get away from being the boss for a couple of hours a day, but still make a few bucks while he played hooky. There were a couple of the drivers I wanted to invite to my wedding, one being my boss Max. Most of them I'd have rather not invited, but I was young and too thin-skinned to face them after the wedding because most of them liked me and several had hinted that they wanted to attend.

So I invited them all, and hoped they'd be on their best behavior.

Jim wanted all of his best high school buddies as groomsmen. That was four dudes. Problem was, I had only three close friends at the time, one of whom was my friend Michael. Michael is a gay man who came out of the closet when we were 21. I didn't think anything about him standing up with me and my bridesmaids, but Jim was worried that some of his older and more conservative relatives might object. When I called my mother for moral support, I was shocked when she expressed some reservations as well. I couldn't figure it out. She loved Michael and she had no problems with him being gay. I am ashamed to admit that at one point during the wedding preparations, I told Michael that he might not be able to stand up with me. He said he understood, but it was obvious he didn't and I didn't blame him. I still don't.

Since I was short on bridesmaids, the only solution I could come up with to even out the bride and groom's sides was to ask my mother to be a bridesmaid. It never occurred to my 22-year-old brain that the "sides" could be uneven and that dumbass arbitrary wedding rules could be thrown out the window. Not only did my mother accept, she behaved as though she had just been crowned the Queen of England.

"*I'll* be the maid of honor," she informed me, and since at that age I was incapable of contradicting her, she indeed became the maid of honor. We decided that since my mother hadn't sewed in years, my friend Jamie, who was also a bridesmaid, would sew Mother's dress as well as her own.

At some point I put my foot down about Michael. I decided that criticism and social mores be damned, my friend Michael would stand up with me in the wedding. I also decided that though he'd be wearing a tuxedo like the rest of the men in the wedding party, he could have a rose colored tie and cummerbund, which would go with my bridesmaid's colors of rose and turquoise. (Cut me a little slack on the colors. It was the early 1990s.)

For a while, I thought everything on the Michael front was going smoothly, until one day he burst out: "Are you making me wear a pink tie and cummerbund because I'm gay?" I honestly hadn't meant it in that way, and I'm not sure why I was so set on the notion of him wearing the rose instead of the turquoise, but now I see his point. When additional grumbling and rumors surfaced about Michael in the wedding, I again phoned my mom to talk it out. I was genuinely distressed. He was my best, most longtime friend. We had been through everything together: all the trials and tribulations of grade school, junior high, high school and college. We'd been through highs and lows, relationships, drinking adventures, pot smoking adventures, parental strife and biggest of all, Michael's coming out.

"I don't understand what the big deal is," I said. Like water breaking through a dam she exploded: "I just don't think it's fair that Michael wants to wear a dress to your wedding!"

And there it was. Even though I'd told her repeatedly that Michael would be wearing a tuxedo, somehow she'd gotten it into her head that he'd be standing up in the wedding ceremony in drag and she had been unable to hear anything else. Never mind that Michael is a gay man, not a drag queen. I explained it again, and for whatever reason, this time she heard me.

"Oh," she said. "Well that's fine then. What's the problem?"

On the day before the wedding, Mother and I went to Jamie's place to pick up Mother's dress. Instead of being grateful that Jamie had done such a beautiful job constructing the garment, Mother was indignant. "Who picked out this pattern for me?" Jamie and I admitted that we'd picked it out together. Mother then pointed to Jamie's dress, hanging on the bedroom door. "Why didn't you make me *that* dress?" We tried to explain that we didn't think that particular dress would be appropriate for her since her body shape was very different from Jamie's. Though my mother was horrible, to her credit, Jamie was gracious.

"Your friend Jamie was terribly rude to me," Mother declared later that day. "That other dress would've been *perfect* for me." It was then that I understood that Mother thought that Jamie was deliberately trying to sabotage her, something that my mother thinks about most women, something she'd warned me repeatedly while I was growing up. "Always remember that female friends will *never* want you to look good," she'd say. "They will purposely compliment you on clothing you look bad in, so that they'll look better than you and pick up more men."

Mother then spent that evening hand-sewing lace cap sleeves onto her dress, as well as an even more bizarre apron with lace trim that she tied on over it. She was so angry about her outfit that in the wedding photos she is visibly bitter, like a chubby, grumpy little cherub with teeny lace wings wearing dewdrop glasses.

The day of the wedding, the day that for most brides is "Me" day, my mother was difficult and critical. Thankfully, her best friend, a woman whom I'd called Aunt Jody since I was a child, showed up to attend the ceremony. I hadn't been expecting her because she hadn't RSVPed, but she provided a welcome buffer between Mother and me, and she offered to drive us to the wedding in her van. As we pulled up to the barn at almost 3 p.m. in the afternoon—as Michael pointed out, the absolute hottest part of the day—I could see the heat waves rising off the hood of Aunt Jody's van. I tried to ignore the fact that the men all looked miserable because I had cruelly insisted on formal dress clothes. While the women could get away with wearing sundresses, the men were sweltering in long sleeves and ties, and the groomsmen were wearing tuxedos. (Seriously, had I been one of those dudes, I would've wanted to strangle me, bride or no bride.) My brother wore the top part of his tuxedo with acid-washed jean shorts. "He's the only smart one," my dad grumbled. I had chosen a tea-length dress so that I wouldn't have a train dragging around the barn, but it still had long sleeves and I was wearing hose. Within minutes my face turned beet red and rivulets of sweat began to run down my cheeks. Jim's face was pink and his hair looked damp, either with hair gel or sweat or both.

I don't remember much of the wedding ceremony. I can't even remember if a wedding march was played. All I know is that something cued me to begin walking and I took off down the aisle as though needing to pass the bouquet off to the next sprinter. I went so fast that halfway down the aisle I stopped and turned around to see my dad hustling toward me because I'd forgotten all about him. The one thing I do remember is Jim holding my hands, looking into my eyes and smiling as though he couldn't believe he was so lucky to be getting married, and of all things, to be marrying me. It was so sweet, and so very him, that I hope I don't forget that moment until the day I die.

The wedding attendees sweltered in the barn, even though a few people had donated their box fans to the event. Nancy told me later that in addition to the heat, here and there people ducked as they were dive-bombed by wasps.

At the reception, which was also at the barn and barely planned because I think I'd envisioned it being a freeform party, Phoebe informed me that she'd had to put the kibosh on several of my coworkers who had begun stuffing their faces at the appetizer buffet even before the ceremony started. One of my aunts, who thought the whole affair was a hoot, made sure to have a photograph of her taken smiling as she stood next to one of the party barn's outhouses, because it had no plumbing. (We rented an additional porta-potty to accommodate everyone.) I was lucky enough to have all four of my grandparents at our wedding, though my grandmother on my dad's side was well into Alzheimer's by that point. Seeing that I was in a wedding dress, she repeatedly came up to me, asked who I was and congratulated me on getting married.

Out on the lawn, the children at the wedding gathered around an antique claw-foot bathtub placed there by the owners as a yard decoration. Apparently the kids had found

59

some toads and decided to sequester them in the bathtub. In their vigorous play, one of the little toads lost a leg, which I know because the daughter of my hippie coworker began to scream in that piercing register of which only little girls are capable: "MY GOD! THEY'RE KILLING THE TOADS! SOMEBODY STOP THEM! THEY'RE PULLING THEIR LEGS OFF!" Normally, I would've stomped over and put a stop to toad-mangling, purposeful or accidental, faster than you can say animal abuse. But on this day, I just couldn't deal. Instead, I continued to smile and exchange pleasantries with the guests, all while sweating my ass off and pretending I was unaware of the carnage going on 30 feet away.

Since it was really too hot to dance, or mingle, or talk or do much of anything, someone suggested that we start opening gifts, I think just to take peoples' minds off the heat. "I have never, ever, seen anyone open gifts at a wedding," Phoebe said, and it wasn't until years later that I could be properly embarrassed by this, because there were so many other things about which to be embarrassed. Finally, someone suggested that we all retire to Jim's sister Nancy's house, as it was large and air conditioned. This caught Nancy off guard. The remains of the great wedding cake project were still strewn across her kitchen and dining room and hadn't been expecting a great horde of guests to invade her home. Again, Jim and I were too young and stupid to understand how imposing we were being. There were about 75 people at the wedding, and thankfully, many of them simply went home. As we were leaving to head to Nancy's, one of Jim's groomsmen approached us. I don't know if he'd been planning to tell us what he did the entire time or if he was inspired by my friend Michael. Nonetheless, as we were loading up our car, Ricky, who now had a long pink earring dangling from one ear said to us, "I just want to let you guys know that I'm gay." We let Ricky know that we were perfectly fine with that and that we supported him, which we did.

When we arrived at Nancy's house, someone turned on the television where most channels were broadcasting OJ Simpson's car chase in his white SUV after the discovery of his murdered ex-wife and her boyfriend. We all watched, transfixed, grateful for the air conditioning.

After the wedding, reviews were mixed. Depending on who you talked to, the wedding was either the best, most fun wedding ever or a total nightmare. Afterward, my friend Phoebe gleefully reenacted my dash down the aisle, pumping her arms up and down. "It was like, *Here comes Amber! Truckin' down the aisle, ready to get herself married.*"

For several years afterward, I dreamed of holding a second wedding as kind of an apology for the first. Somewhere indoors and climate controlled. Someplace that we could decorate tastefully and maybe have the food catered in. But many of the people who attended I haven't spoken to in years, nor would I want to. Jim's parents are both gone, as are all of my grandparents. I am still friends with Phoebe, Jamie and Michael, but there's no way in hell my mother would ever again be my bridesmaid.

Savory Salmon Cheesecake

At our wedding, we provided a table of substantial appetizers, crackers, cheeses, dips and veggies and the like. In place of expensive cheeses, Phoebe suggested that we bake a couple of savory cheesecakes that could be eaten with fresh vegetables and crackers. This worked really well; they were indeed much less expensive than purchasing cheese wheels and they tasted wonderful. Phoebe made these look pretty with fresh herbs and vegetables. It was so long ago it's hard to remember and the only wedding I've ever attended where I didn't eat much because I was such a nervous wreck. I do remember that Phoebe hollowed out a couple of squashes and cabbages to hold the dips which was extremely Martha-esque of her. But then, she's good at things like that.

Smoked Salmon Cheesecake
1/4 cup plain dry bread crumbs
3 eight-ounce packages of cream cheese, softened
3 large eggs
½ cup sour cream (light is okay)
2 Tbsp flour
1 ½ tsp grated lemon zest
4 oz sliced smoked salmon, coarsely chopped
6 scallions, thinly sliced
4 Tbsp chopped fresh dill
1 Tbsp capers, chopped
Salt and pepper to taste

Method: Heat oven to 325°F. Coat bottom and sides of an 8 inch springform pan with nonstick spray. Add bread crumbs; tilt and rotate pan to cover bottom and sides with crumbs. Beat cream cheese in a large bowl with mixer on medium speed 1 minute or just until smooth. Beat in eggs, 1 at a time, until blended. Beat in sour cream, flour, zest, salt and pepper until combined. Stir in salmon, scallions, dill and capers. Pour into prepared pan and smooth the top with a rubber spatula if necessary. Bake 40 minutes or until center is just set. Remove pan to wire rack to cool completely. Refrigerate until ready to serve. Shortly before serving, remove sides of springform pan.

My X-Rated Dad

When my dad's second wife divorced him, he went through a period of darkness. He was still teaching art classes at the local college, so he had his students to bring some light to his life, but otherwise, he sort of floundered aimlessly for a couple of years, not really knowing what to do with himself. For the first time that I could remember, he didn't seem to have the heart to take his glass blowing seriously, so after a few months he decided to revisit his hobby of taking photos of naked women, a pastime that he'd given up a few years into his first marriage. After all, he was once again a freewheeling bachelor with no woman in his life to regulate this behavior, so why not? At first, he recruited life drawing models for tasteful photo shoots and was even invited by a couple of galleries to show his collections of nudes. At some point, though, a local stripper asked him to take photos of her for her portfolio. She ended up liking his work and told a stripper friend, who told another stripper friend, and so on, and before he knew it, Dad was up to his eyeballs in tits and ass and had provided photos for the portfolios of nearly every stripper in the tri-city area. (Yes, strippers have portfolios; most are trying to make it to the "big time," which, for strippers, means Vegas.)

Since, when his second wife left, she took with her any sort of decorating aesthetic in the home, Dad did what most bachelors do, which was to put any damn thing that struck his fancy anywhere he pleased. This included a hodgepodge of the many objects d'art he'd collected over the years; furniture salvaged from the divorce, curbsides and dumpsters; and now, photos of naked women. After just a couple of years, the naked women had taken over the house, until there were naked women in the dining room, the living room, the bathroom—but not as many as you'd think in the bedroom. They appeared in the basement, the garage and his glassblowing studio. Some of them are totally nude, while others wear lingerie or maybe some intriguing prop like a string of pearls. I've told him many times that it would be nice if I could bring our child's grade school classes out to his place for glassblowing field trips, but I can't because of all the naked photos all over the place.

"What's the big deal?" he always says, looking at me as though *I'm* the one with the problem. "Naked people never hurt anybody."

A few years into this newfound naked-o-rama, Dad retired from his professorship at the university and then began to bitch and moan that he wanted a Harley Davidson motorcycle. Only he never did anything about it, because my dad is notoriously cheap. He's one of those people who's socked away his retirement not by making bucketloads of money, but by turning off lights, keeping the air-conditioning at 80 degrees, the heat at 60, and showering once a week. He rarely shops for clothes, and most of his t-shirts—many of which are 30-plus years old—look as though they've been washed with rocks and old newspapers.

65

He drove one of his vehicles over 300 thousand miles, putting two new engines and three transmissions into it before sending it out to pasture. After a couple of years of his wistfully wishing that a Harley Davidson motorcycle would somehow drop out of the sky and into his life, I finally said, "*Jesus*, Dad. Just buy the damn motorcycle already. You have the money. You're retired. Enjoy yourself a little. What are you gonna do? Die with all that money in the bank?" I remember him staring at me dumbfounded, blinking a few times as if I'd thumped him between the eyes with my thumb and forefinger. It was as if the notion of prying open his wallet and *purchasing* a motorcycle had never even entered his thoughts.

The Harley acquisition not only made him immensely happy in-and-of itself, but it also introduced him to the world of bikers, a group of people who share Dad's worldview on politics, life and sexuality. Bikers are, for the most part, politically conservative, but they enjoy public displays of drinking, nudity, sex and general debauchery. They are often intensely pro-U.S.A., pro-flag, pro-military and anti- anything liberal, high-brow, 'elite' or wussy. They are, Dad insists, the salt of the earth and would give anybody the red, white and blue eagle t-shirts off their sweaty, beer-soaked backs. I believe him.

I think buying the Harley created so much joy for Dad that he then decided to add a full-sized antique John Deer tractor to his menagerie, which reminded him of his childhood on the farm and which he could occasionally back out of the shed and fart around on, on his two acres of property.

In addition to the new biker hobby, Dad continued to make inroads to the world of adult entertainment, networking with people in the sex industry, which lead him to become an investor in a "gentlemen's club." When the deal first went through, and my husband mentioned his father-in-law's new venture to his boss, Chuck, who also happens to be a good friend, Chuck called me, laughing his ass off with the knowledge that my brother Clay and I might someday become equal seven-and-a-half percent owners in a titty bar somewhere in Missouri when Dad kicks the bucket. (I've never actually seen it, but Clay has, so I know it exists.)

Eventually, through some sort of bizarre alignment of the heavens, Dad's photography, biker and naked girl hobbies converged and the next thing I knew, my father was being given press passes to biker rallies and adult entertainment industry functions. He shows up with his press pass and his camera, taking photos to his heart's content, and then sells the photos to biker, tattoo and sex-industry magazines.

I honestly don't think my father could be happier or more satisfied with his life.

Besides the biker rallies, which he loves, the one event he looks forward to all year long is Nudes-A-Poppin in Indiana. (There is officially no apostrophe on the 'n' at the end of "poppin.")

Really? I hear you asking yourself. *Nudes-A-Poppin?* Yes, it's true. Nudes-A-Poppin is a contest for showgirls and show-guys, and, as the name implies, the contestants are all-nude, all weekend long, and the event is held outdoors. In the middle of summer. In Indiana. It's an event that, in the past, has drawn celebrities like Vern Troyer (Mini Me from the Austin Powers films) and Gene Simmons of the band Kiss. Dad has photos of himself with both of them. It's also an event where clothing is optional for everyone involved, including the spectators. Prizes are given in categories such as "Ms. Nude Entertainer" and "Mr. Nude North America" and "Ms. Nude Rising Star." While covering Nudes-A-Poppin, Dad stays at the nudist camp that sponsors the event. I guess I *could* imagine my father "hanging out" as it were, just talking with folks, playing volley ball and swimming, but I try not to.

"I don't know why people are so hung up on nudity," he says, often. "Everybody at the nudist camp is naked all the time, and nobody thinks anything about it. Men, women, little kids, grammas and grandpas. People recognize me there now. It's just great!"

Sometimes Dad arranges for his photo shoots of models and strippers to take place out in the country; he has a deep appreciation for the subtle beauty of Kansas and finds that a naked woman goes very nicely against a bale of hay, a field of sunflowers, a dilapidated barn, or a rusty piece of old farm equipment. Since his place is a little way out of town and he's got a couple of acres with some nice gardens, sometimes he does the photo shoots there. His neighbors to the north, whose house is quite close to his, have two small children. Dad says he's spoken with the young couple next door, though, and insists that they don't mind that he occasionally has lovely nude vixens frolicking in his yard.

One afternoon, Dad called me to relay the news from his place, which I've come to think of as Raunch Ranch.

"Well, your hedonistic father had a great time this afternoon."

"Oh yeah?" I said, bracing for what might come next. "Why's that?"

"I had two girls out here at my place wanting their pictures taken, again." (I knew that in my dad's central Kansas farmspeak, "again" means that two *new* girls had come out to his property to strip for photos, not women who had been there previously.)

"Really," I said.

"Yep. And they're not one bit self-conscious." My dad often remarks on the free-spiritedness of the young naked women he photographs, as though he considers it a mark of good character. "They just took their clothes off and the one girl jumped on the tractor and the other one got on the bike. If I'd known that women were so attracted to Harleys and tractors I would've bought them years ago."

Sometimes he emails his photos to me, for a couple of reasons, if I had to guess. For one thing, he wants me to be in the loop as to what's going on his life, and for another, he delights in attempting to embarrass his children, the result of which has made us both *extremely* resilient to humiliation. In one email, Dad described the women in the attached photo as "a sweet grandmother, daughter, and granddaughter I met this weekend." He added that since the photo would be appearing in a biker magazine, I was to please not forward the photo to anyone else. Sure enough, in the photo is a young-looking grandma with flowers painted around her nipples, standing next to her daughter, whose nipples are pierced, standing next to *her* daughter, who looks as though she can't be more than eighteen and whose nipples are pierced with even larger gage hoops than her mother's.

Ah, family.

While many people would be horrified by their fathers' forays into such cringe-worthy activities, I'm happy he's found his stride and hasn't married a third time, since I'm fairly certain it wouldn't last, anyway. He's making a multitude of friends, keeping himself busy in his retirement years, and as a bonus, the friends section of his Facebook page looks like a pinup calendar. Not bad for a guy who's soon to be 70.

Besides. I learned years ago that to be embarrassed by anyone in my family is a huge waste of time.

Kansas Red Beer

Ingredients:
1 can cheap-ass American beer (Miller, Coors, PBR, Keystone ... doesn't matter, they all taste the same.)
½ cup tomato juice or V8 or Clamato or bloody Mary mix
Assorted spices and flavorings to suit your taste

Method:
Pour beer into a tall, clear glass. Tilt the glass and slowly add tomato juice or tomato beverage of your choice. Feel free to add to your taste any combination of Worcestershire sauce, garlic powder, garlic salt (watch out for foaming!), lime juice, lemon juice, green olive juice or hot pepper sauce like Tobasco. Mix gently with a spoon.

Enjoy on a hot night on the front porch with your family or friends and a flyswatter.

Red beer is a controversial, but traditional, drink in Kansas and much of the Midwest. I've heard people say that to drink a red beer ruins both the beer and the tomato juice. I disagree. My dad gave me my first sip of red beer when I was just a kid, maybe 7 or 8 years old, and I was instantly hooked. While I like bloody Marys, they always taste sort of tinny to me. A red beer on the other hand is like a refreshing cold soup. Or something like that.

Healthy as a Horse, Stubborn as a Mule

My dad's immune system was forged in the cow-pee ponds of Central Kansas. As a boy growing up on a wheat and cattle farm outside the tiny town of Holyrood in the 1950s, he was exposed to poultry, hogs, milk cows, beef cattle, and all of the dung and bacteria that come with said livestock. Until he was in high school, their family's only toilet was the outhouse out back of the house. He rose early and worked long hours outdoors only to end his days sleeping in an un-air conditioned, unheated upstairs farmhouse bedroom. On the most brutal of summer days, he and his brother could either take a cool dip in the galvanized tank from which the cattle drank, one of the pasture ponds in which the cattle bathed, peed and shit, or the dubious swimming hole down the road. (If you've ever experienced a river, pond or lake in Kansas, you know that they're nearly always murky brown, smell of dead fish and often conceal a giant catfish or snapping turtle that could and would remove one of your toes.)

As a result, for most of his life, my father was rarely ever sick. He's getting older though, and he's begun to slow down and fall apart as humans do. So when he does require medical attention, his denial is epic. He hates admitting his fallibilities, as this might somehow translate to weakness. He doesn't care for medical staff, despises the "liberal" institution of Medicare and thinks that for a man to seek out any sort of health care is to admit that he might be pussified.

In his 50s, when his eyes began to go bad, he refused to make an appointment with an optometrist. Instead, he purchased the cheap, non-prescription magnifying reading glasses available in most drug stores. He'd put them on whenever he needed to look at something in detail. I remember one particular time when he was working on the faulty toilet in the house that my friends and I rented from him while in college. While bent over the toilet, he turned to look at me with his magnified, Mr. Magoo eyes and said, *"Amber, this is a puzzler like I've never seen,"* much to my roommates' delight, who then repeated the phrase for weeks. Dad bought stronger and stronger glasses from the drug store until one day, he found that he'd maxed them out. Only then did he go to an eye doctor.

Once, while cleaning out the gutters of said rental house, he fell off the roof. Though the hospital was only two blocks away, he crawled to his van to drive himself home, where he lie for a few days moaning, face down, on a mattress in the middle his living room. To this day, I'm not sure who dragged the mattress out to the living room for him, or if it was just there and that was where he landed. In the mornings before going to work, I'd bring him breakfast casseroles and beg him to see a doctor.

"Damn women!" he yelled at me one morning, because his girlfriend at the time had also been on his case to see a doctor. He'd raise his head and arms a few inches off the mattress to prove that he was getting better, all on his own. "See? See?!" he'd yell. Then collapse in agony, flat on his face.

When Dad finally did go to the hospital three days later, they immediately put his leg in a cast to squeeze the bones back into place because, though x-rays didn't reveal that anything was broken, some of the bones had been knocked askew. A full year later when walking was still difficult and he was in considerable pain, Dad made an appointment with a sports doctor who x-rayed the bottom of his foot and found that his heel bone *had* broken, but the bones had already fused back together incorrectly, so that there was nothing to be done to fix it. Dad limps to this day, his foot full of arthritis.

When he entered his mid-60s, Dad tried for several months to ignore the strange flutters he felt in his heart, but eventually decided that maybe this was something to have a professional look at. I can't tell you the name of his heart disorder, because he can't tell me. Per his doctor's orders, he takes blood thinners to keep his blood from pooling in his heart, and he's supposed to get his blood drawn and the drug dosage adjusted at regular intervals. But he refuses to do this because he is convinced that his doctor is just trying to cheat Medicare. One summer morning while weeding his vegetable garden, his heart began to beat irregularly and he passed out. He told me he wasn't worried, though, because he checked his watch and determined that he was probably only out for a few seconds, maybe a couple of minutes at the most.

There was the evening that he called me from Wichita, which is about two-and-a-half hours away from our home town of

Lawrence, where he'd gone on business. He'd been getting ready to settle down for the night when suddenly, he lost his vision in one eye.

When he told me, I shifted into panic mode. I insisted he call a cab and have it drive him to the emergency room, thinking he might be having a stroke.

"But I was just going to bed," he said. "I thought I'd drive myself to the hospital in the morning." His forced cavalierness about the whole thing pissed me off. If he was that unconcerned, I thought, he never would have bothered to call me. As a compromise, he drove himself to the emergency room. After dark, with one working eye. And maybe having a stroke. I hoped he wouldn't take out a busload of nuns on the way.

It turned out to be detached retina. Luckily, a competent eye surgeon was able to tack the faulty retina to the back of his eyeball with a laser the next morning and Dad recovered his sight completely.

(It was thrilling to hear Dad describe the procedure, which involves putting you out briefly, at which time the doctor pops your eyeball out of its socket. Apparently you then come-to with your eyeball resting on your cheek, but you don't know this because you can't see out of that eye anyway. Your hands are restrained so that you don't absentmindedly reach up to brush your face and in so doing, harm your eyeball. Then they clamp your head in a vice so that you can't move and they work on the eye while you're awake. Then they knock you out again to put the eyeball back into place. The attending nurse told Dad that the first time she watched the procedure, she fainted dead away.)

You'd think that after losing sight in one's eye, one might be tempted to take immediate action upon becoming totally deaf in one ear. But apparently, there's no need to panic. All one has to do is go to one's local health food co-op, purchase an ear candle, call one's daughter while en route to her house, lie down in the middle of her living room and ask said daughter to light the candle, since logistically, one can't do that oneself. I thought that either my husband Jim's head would explode or he'd bust a gut trying to hold in the laughter at the sight of my Dad with a burning candle in his hear whilst lying in the middle of our living room. Dad had brought a paper plate with a hole cut into it to place the candle into to catch any candle wax that might spill, and I thought far enough in advance to put a towel under his head just in case the wax dripped off the plate. But I was completely unprepared when the candle had burned down to a nub and I had no idea how to put the flame out. Ear candles are basically paper cones dipped in wax. There's no wick, and the candle burns messily, producing an excess of flame and ash. My mind raced trying to figure out how to put out the flame: *Throw water at it? No. I could go get a towel and beat the flame out. No. Too messy. Oh shit! Burning embers fluttering everywhere! Could catch living room on fire! Must stop this now!* So I did the only think I could think of, which was to blow at the candle, which did put it out, but caused burning embers fly around the room.

"Why didn't you just carry it to the kitchen sink?" Jim asked, disgusted, as I carefully gathered the flaky embers.

Dad stood up, snapping his thick fingers next to his ear. But he could hear nothing.

"Maybe it doesn't work right away," he mused. "Maybe I just need to give it a couple of days."

"Maybe you need to go see a doctor," I snapped. At that point I was kind of pissed and embarrassed for both of us.

A couple of days later Dad called, bragging that he could once again hear out of that ear.

There was the weekend I went to Wichita for my high school reunion, and Dad called me the day I got back. I was tired from the drive, lack of sleep and too much alcohol, and listened to his story without much sympathy or alarm. He said he'd fallen outside his glass studio, a stand-alone building on his property, and had thought for a moment that maybe he'd broken a hip because he sensed pain in his leg. But after a few moments he decided he was fine. Until he looked at his leg a couple of minutes after that and saw that his sock was soaked with blood. Only then did he understand that the piece of angle-iron he'd fallen on—"angle-arn" he calls it—had cut his leg.

Rather than call someone to drive him to the hospital, which is clear across town from his house, he drove himself to the emergency room. He managed to make it through the emergency room doors and passed out. To this day, he has no idea how long he was unconscious, but suspects that it may have been as long as an hour.

The hospital staff subjected him to several scans and x-rays, as hospitals are want to do. Dad told me he protested valiantly, accusing the hospital staff of performing unnecessary procedures until they gave up, stitched up the wound and released him. They wanted him to call someone to drive him home, but he didn't want to. Having dealt with Dad before, the staff knew it was pointless to argue with him. They did, however, give him explicit instructions to go straight home and rest.

As the orderlies wheeled him out to his car, the front desk nurse called out: "Is he still as stubborn as he always was?" The orderlies confirmed that yes, he was.

Despite the order to go straight home, this was the weekend of the Lake Perry Biker Rally, and Dad *never* misses the Lake Perry Biker Rally. So he drove himself from the emergency room to the lake. After standing in the beer line for a few minutes, Dad dropped to the ground like a sack of flour. Medics descended on him, bringing him back to consciousness. They wanted to load him up in the ambulance and take him back to the hospital.

"Hell, no!" Dad told them, and went to sit in the tent with the Christian bikers, who, in all their goodness and godliness, made sure he stayed hydrated with water, not beer.

As I said, Dad relayed this story to me over the phone. But in the initial telling, he didn't include the detail about the "angle-arn" having plunged so deep into his thigh that it touched bone. So I was under the impression that he'd received a bad cut, lost a lot of blood, and was now stitched up and doing fine. Until he came to visit me.

He came hobbling up our steep driveway, taking one pronounced, normal step with his good leg, wincing, and then dragging the other leg a few inches. The whole procedure was obviously an exercise in pain, and it looked as if it were going to be impossible for him to get up our front steps and then up the stairs to the living room, but he managed to do it.

Since it was still summer and we live in Kansas, he was wearing shorts, which meant that nothing was left to the imagination. The affected leg was swelled up twice its normal size, and in addition to the jagged black stitches, most of his upper leg had turned some shade of blue or black. Making it to the living room, he collapsed in a chair.

"Do you want something to put your leg up on?" I asked.

"That would be nice," he said.

"Are you *supposed* to have your leg up?" I asked, fitting an ottoman under his foot.

"Yes. I'm also supposed to be putting ice on it four times a day for twenty minutes at a time."

"*Dad* ..." I said, but he cut me off.

"I've been busy. I had things to do. I haven't had a chance to sit down today."

"Did they prescribe you some sort of pain killer?"

"No. I don't do drugs."

"Are you on antibiotics?"

"No. *I told them I don't do drugs.*"

"Dad. Your leg was *stabbed* with a piece of rusty old metal."

"They washed the wound out," he barked, and I knew that was the end of the conversation.

We made small talk then, and he watched some television, which he likes to do at my house since he refuses to pay for cable or a satellite dish at his house.

As he was leaving I said, "Dad, stay home tomorrow. With your leg up. Please."

"Okay," he croaked.

79

As he made his way to his truck, he'd grab the bad leg with his hands and manually haul it along like a small corpse. It occurred to me that he shouldn't be driving, even though it was the good leg he used to work the gas pedal. Dad favors manual transmission vehicles, so I knew the bad leg would be operating the clutch. With a misty rain beginning to soak my clothes, I knocked on his car window, which was streaked with moisture. He rolled it down and I offered to drive him home in his car. Jim could follow to give me a ride back to our house, I said.

As per usual, he refused. As I watched his truck roll off into the night on the water-glazed roads, I crossed my fingers that he wouldn't lose control of his vehicle and kill someone.

The next day, much to my surprise and relief, Dad went to see his doctor who did prescribe him a pain killer and an antibiotic, and he took them.

Being a glassblower, Dad has sustained countless burns over the course of his adult life, most of which are second- and third-degree, and none of which he's ever sought medical care for. One Thanskgivng celebration Dad stood over the spread on his kitchen table and pointed with a kitchen knife to a perfectly round, full-to-bursting blister at the tip of one of his big fingers. The little dome was milky white and I wouldn't have been surprised if I'd leaned in closer to see a tiny little snowman inside, glitter alighting on its little hat. "Look at that," he said, gesturing with the point of the knife dangerously close to the blister. "Burned myself the other day." All I could think about was the knife coming in contact with the blister and our Thanksgiving dinner being covered in spooge.

Dad scolds me from time to time, saying that I don't call often enough.

"One day I'll wake up dead," he says, "and you won't even know it. I'll lay there for a month before you bother to check on me."

Because that would be *my* fault.

Author's note: My dad and I disagree about the sequence of events after he fell off the roof and injured his leg. He insists that he went directly to the hospital, was put in a walking boot cast and went home to lie on the mattress in the living room. One morning, when he tried to go downstairs to his bedroom, he says he slipped and fell down the stairs. That's honestly not how I remember things, so I've kept the narrative as I originally wrote it.

Chili Relleno Casserole

I got this recipe from a cookbook my Grammy (Villis) gave me and it's the recipe I used to make Dad's breakfast casserole when he broke his foot. It's fatty, but *excellent*.

Ingredients:
2 large cans sliced green chilis, drained
6 beaten eggs with 1 tablespoon milk
1 cup grated Cheddar cheese
1 cup grated Jack cheese

Method: Preheat oven to 350 degrees.

Spread ½ the chilies on the bottom of an oiled pie pan (a glass one works nicely), then half the cheese then half the egg mix. Repeat. Bake for about 45 minutes, or until a knife inserted in the center of the casserole comes out clean. I like to sprinkle a little garlic powder and dried oregano into the egg mixture before baking.

Serves 4-6

I Love Geeks

You may not be curious about what gets a pale, pudgy, middle-aged writer all hot-and-bothered, but I'm going to tell you anyway. I love geeks. <u>Love</u> them. Now, I did not know this about myself for the first few years of my life. It took awhile to figure it out, which I did about the tail-end of my senior year of high school. My tastes in men haven't changed all that much since.

After spending my teenage years lusting after most persons male and alive, I settled on the fact that I prefer men who are computer, science, engineering or math geeks. I believe that I am attracted to these types of men because they are versed in a world that I can't even begin to comprehend, so this makes them—and therefore the workings of their minds—tantalizingly out of reach. I think I imagine my ideal of the male heterosexual geek to be the epitome of still waters that run deep. I'm convinced that somewhere inside that sweet nerdy guy is a bubbling cauldron of testosterone, sweat and sperm just waiting for his Princess Leia or Lieutenant Uhura to let it out.

There's something so underdogishly attractive about all those soft-spoken guys with the big minds who played D&D, read Douglas Adams novels and got pushed around in high school. They ended up being relevant in society, as opposed to the high school quarterback or the prom king or the guy voted most likely to succeed. That's not to say that the prom king isn't successful. He's probably doing well in real estate or car sales or maybe he's a chiropractor or owns his own restaurant. All very noble and necessary pursuits, but let's face it: these days, it's the geeks who run the world. They could literally put us all back in the dark ages if they wanted to. Doctors may save lives, but it's the geeks who've advanced medicine's equipment. For millions of years it was the tough guys who carved out a safe niche for the human race, but now it's the geeks who make sure we have clean water, power when we flip the switch, climate-controlled cars and jets that fly themselves. It's geeks who have taken the human race to the stars, to the depths of the Earth's oceans and geeks who will be the ones to figure out clean, alternative energies that will take us into the next century. It's geeks who have given us flat-screen televisions, iPods, laptops, smart phones, e-readers and damn near everything that makes Western existence convenient and fun.

I have no interest in bad boys, or the guy with the muscular neck and the six pack abs, or doctors, or businessmen—who pretty much make me want to puke—and I certainly have no interest in being with another word-nerd like myself. How annoying would it be to have two people blathering about 'voice' and 'character development' in the same house? Blech.

Me, I like a man who knows his way around a scientific calculator and has Linux installed on his PC. I like a man who's into the latest techie gadgetry, meteorology, Stephen Hawking, first-person video games (but not *that* into first-person video games), science and nature documentaries, and Tolkien. I like a man who carries a messenger bag, speaks binary, is into Star Wars (but not *that* into Star Wars), and who's tickled pink when yet another Weird Al Yankovic album comes out. A man who'll get up early in the morning to watch a space launch or stay up late to watch a meteor shower. I like a man who can get us where we're going with his GPS, set up my Kindle, back up my laptop files, format my hard drive and save me from the dreaded blue screen of death by retrieving my memory from the dump file.

The fates coded a perfect match when I met my future husband Jim as a sophomore in college. He was the manager of the grocery store where I worked, which meant that he was responsible and level-headed. None of the other girls who worked in the store would date him because, they said, he was too *nice*. He was smart, polite, and most importantly, he was majoring in computer science. So while the other girls were busy chasing after their drinking, toking, motorcycle riding bad boys, I went after my Nissan-driving, *Castle Wolfenstein* playing geek.

Occasionally, Jim will have to call tech support for one of the gadgets in our house and I like to listen in on the conversations because it's titillating. The conversation always starts with the person on the other end talking to my husband as though he's just another dumbass with some inane problem that's obviously caused by operator error. "Yeah, yeah," he'll say impatiently, and then he'll throw out a couple of techie code words so the person on the other end of the phone knows that he or she is speaking to a fellow geek, and that's when the conversation gets *really* exciting. Because instead of having to walk some novice through fifteen minutes worth of baby steps, Jim and the other tech-head can get the heart of the problem within seconds. Sometimes, the conversation goes particularly well and I can hear the geek respect flowing both ways. Other times, Jim will be speaking with an inferior geek, his eyes periodically rolling at the moronity of it all. These conversations are *the best*, because I love to hear my husband flex his technical biceps. "Idiots," he'll say, and hang up the phone. By that point my underpants are in a wad and I'm itching to tear off his clothes.

Less often, I'll get to hang around with Jim and his geek friends, and their conversation gets me worked up into a froth. They throw around terms like compiler, Linux, dot-net, operator, Ubuntu, crapplet, PHP, algorithm and the sexiest geek term of all: raspberry pi.

Nothing bums me out more than when my husband says he's not the smartest geek he knows. "I'm not a real coder," he'll say. "I just kind of hack things together."

Shhhhh. You're ruining my fantasy.

Moving Mom

There are times in life when we must face our worst fears: A cancer scare. The unexpected death of someone close. Being dumped by that boyfriend or girlfriend whom we knew was just a little out of our league and was dating us just to avoid being single and whom we also knew, sooner or later, was going to move on to someone "better."

Ever since I moved away from home at the age of eighteen, one of my biggest fears has been that my mother will move in with me. Sometime in the spring of 2000, I received the call from my mother I'd been dreading. "My landlord is kicking me out," she said, and my stomach dropped to my knees. Her voice was low and bedraggled and she said she was in shock. I don't remember now exactly how long the landlord gave her to evacuate the house she was living in, but it wasn't long … about a month, maybe a month and a half. She'd done to that house what she's done to her current one—planted her jungle-like gardens all over the corner lot, eclipsing the yard with wild masses of greenery, tangled vines and flowers, and filled the house with her menagerie of crap. Piecing together her side of the story, I had a suspicion that one day, perhaps while attempting mow around the morass outside, or after he'd waded through her packed basement to look at the fuse box, her landlord had decided enough was enough.

"I'll be moving in with you," she announced. "Figure out where you want the grass killed in your yard. That's where I'll put my pots of flowers." Her plan was to live with us until she could find a place to rent in Lawrence, because she "Wanted to be closer to her kids." Being that rent prices were much higher in Lawrence than in Wichita where she was living, and that she was nearly destitute as far as cash was concerned, and considering all the stuff she owned, and the fact that she also had two cats and a dog, I knew that the prospect of her finding a place to rent in Lawrence, where the rental market is geared toward college students and well-off retirees, was pretty piss-poor. I could see what was coming. She'd move in with us and maybe never move out.

Now I was in shock. I was also trapped like a rat. I couldn't tell my mother that she couldn't move in with me. I just couldn't. On the other hand, I couldn't let her move in with me because to do so would be the end of my marriage. The first five or so years we were together, Jim tried to get along with his mother in law. He really did. Eventually, after her endless string of put-downs, cold shoulders and borderline hostility, he stopped trying to be friends and became cordial but distant. Once when Mother was staying with us and spied one of Jim's C++ computer programming books on the coffee table, she picked it up, glanced at it, tossed it back on the table and asked,

"What's *he* reading? Computers for dummies?" She made sure to say this loud enough for him to hear a couple of rooms away.

"I can't figure out why Jim and I don't get along," my mother said to me another time. At that point, I was still routinely baffled by her behavior and hopeful that she could change, so the comment was like hot sauce on a paper cut. *Really, Sherry? You just* can't *figure it out?*

After her call, I couldn't sleep at night. I couldn't think during the day at my job as a reporter for the small newspaper where I worked. I started having honest-to-god panic attacks. After a week or so, I had a revelation: if there wasn't a rental place available for her, I could make one available. I could take some money I'd set aside for our retirement, convince my brother to donate some money to the cause, put a down payment on a modest house and let her make the house payment. I knew that what I was asking my little brother to do was wrong, but it was the only thing I could think to do. The only way I could figure out how to preserve my little corner of sanity.

We quickly figured out that there was no real estate in Lawrence that fit into our price range. Twenty minutes down the road in Topeka was another story. We bought a two-bedroom house made in the 1940s with a basement and a detached garage, on a corner lot with a large yard. Plenty of room for Mother, her animals, her gardens and all her stuff.

As I worked out the details and made the arrangements I also began to feel something else along with the panic: Hope. Somehow I'd gone from being the laziest teenager on the planet to doer- and problem fixer extraordinaire in my 20s and 30s.

89

Getting shit done made me stupid-high. (In my 40s, I'm starting to get over that.) I thought that a new house, a new town and distance from her own mother would mean a new start for my mom. Maybe she would take up watercolor painting again. Maybe she would date. Maybe she'd ease up on her hypochondria. Maybe she'd stop obsessing about Dad. Maybe a move would mean shedding the past and getting rid of a lot of physical and mental shit. Maybe she could actually be happy. And then maybe I could be happy too.

I made the 2-hour drive from Lawrence to Wichita the two weekends before Mom's big move to help her pack. It was a surreal experience, sitting in the middle of Mom's things, filling and taping shut boxes yet making very little progress in reducing the mounds of stuff into manageable cardboard cubes. As we worked, my mother at a snail's pace, every forty-five minutes or so she'd say: "Why don't we take a break?" or "We should rest for a while. We've been working hard." It was a mantra I'd heard much of my life. For many years, I'd gone along with it, but no longer. "Resting doesn't get things done," I'd remind her, and continue to pack.

The second time I made the drive, I found my mother sitting on her front porch fanning herself with a magazine, with about a tenth of her belongings surrounding her, the only things she could bear to part with. She was supposedly holding a sale. Most of the porch-sale consisted of her hoochie wardrobe from her going-out days in the 1980s. But the '80s fashions weren't back in style yet, so they were not big sellers. She was also selling plant-starts from her yard in paper cups for one dollar each and a few trinkets that were placed just-so on tables. I remember being viscerally frustrated by the piddling amount of her things she'd chosen to part with, versus the piles of what to me, was absolute junk. I wanted nothing more than to load up at least half of it and drive it all to a dump. Not being able to do so made me anxious and angry. More importantly, while she was running her little sham of a yard sale, she was not packing. I hope I went inside and packed. I honestly don't remember. Maybe I bought into her denial and sat on the porch with her. Over the years, we've had a lot of denial parties together, my mother and I. What I do remember is my mother having a delightful time greeting people as they wandered up the driveway and onto the porch. She'd chat them up and encourage them not so much to buy her things as the plant starts. "If there's some sort of plant or flower that you're looking for that you don't see here, just let me know. I probably have it. We can go dig it up!"

When the porch sale was over and hardly anything had sold, did my mother put those things on the curb for the trash men to dispose of? Of course not. She drug it all back inside to be packed. When I left her a week before the move, hugging and saying good bye, I remember having serious doubts that she'd be packed when I returned a week later. *But she has be*, my inner voice nagged. *Because what would happen if she weren't?*

At first my mother had chosen the second-to-last weekend in May to move, but then she rethought the matter and asked her landlord if she could stay one more week to vacate the property Memorial Day weekend. This would give us an extra day for the move. "Maybe we'll drive down and join you just for fun," my sister-in-law Nancy said before Jim, Clay and I left to help. By "we" she meant herself and her husband

David. She then told me a story about the moving day she and David helped David's parents move. Only when they'd arrived, the house wasn't packed, so they'd had to spend the entire day packing before they could even begin to help with the actual moving. The story made my skin crawl. Was I willfully ignoring the obvious with my mother? I shoved the feelings away. My mother had to be packing, diligently and with furrowed brow, because ... well, because.

When Jim, Clay and I arrived with the Brobdingnagian moving van my mother had reserved, the house looked much as it had the last time I'd seen her. Ninety percent of the house wasn't packed. Two bedrooms, a living room, a bathroom, a kitchen and a whole basement, still full. Still full and not packed. Dismay is not the word for what I felt. Betrayal was closer. At that moment, I was done tiptoeing around Sherry's feelings. I looked her straight in the face and asked her what the hell she was thinking.

"What?" she asked, blinking like an innocent child.

"*What?*" I yelled at her. "Mom, look at this place. This *sucks*!"

She looked at me levelly. "I did my best," she said. It was her "mother" voice, the one that indicated her word was final and we wouldn't be discussing the matter anymore.

My mother hired six movers to pack the moving van. When they arrived, a couple of the guys who seemed to be in charge came into the house and glanced around with uncomfortable confusion. Mother instructed them to start hauling out the furniture first, and my mother owns an unwarranted amount of large furniture considering she is a single tiny woman. In the meantime, she told them, the rest of us would work on packing the smaller items.

Sometime during the afternoon, my brother and sister in law showed up. Nancy gawped at me with a look of horror mixed with the glint of an insane smile that said, *If we don't laugh about this, we're all going to cry* and *I can't believe this is happening to us again.*

It was a long, hard day. It was hot and humid outside, but the air conditioning was off because the front and back door were open while the men hauled stuff to the moving truck. As we sweated and worked through the layers of crap in the living room and toward the kitchen, I realized how unaware I had been about the state of my mother's house and thus, the state of her mind. The kitchen was buried in dirty dishes. There was no time to wash anything, so we wrapped up the dishes, dried food and all, and packed them. But the cabinets and drawers were still crammed full. My mother owns three or four sets of service for twelve, including all the accoutrements like gravy boats and butter dishes, enough silverware to accommodate the dinner hour at a soup kitchen, and enough pots and pans to supply a restaurant. As we made our way down through the madness to the bare counter-tops and floors, I remember pitching rotten food and even a half-consumed gallon of curdled milk that lie forgotten under a pile of souring rags in the corner.

The basement was worse. In addition to the boxes and boxes of moldy books and magazines, there were dirty furnace filters and trash bags full of dirty kitty litter lying around. I'd heard of stories like this, but couldn't comprehend how it had happened here. Growing up, my mother had always insisted on a tidy house, and somehow she'd gotten her way, despite the fact that my brother and I were unmotivated little shits who were never much help.

We opened cabinet after cabinet and drawer after drawer stuffed with trinkets and multiples of crafting supplies as well as plain old junk she'd salvaged from anyone and everyone. In the living room was a heavy armoire that my mother had padlocked shut. We had to wait while she located the key so that we could pack whatever was so valuable inside. When opened we found a hundred cheap, Chinese-made bud vases that had probably cost her 25 cents apiece. Mother insisted that these be individually wrapped and packed in a marked box.

In one of the bedrooms was an entire line of Rug Rats dolls that Mother had taken out of the packages. But she'd saved the packages, convinced that she could put the dolls back in, making them worth a fortune someday. During the packing, someone tried to throw the boxes away, but Mother went out to the trash and dug them back out. In fact, she dug a lot of things out of the trash and brought them back into the house. Everyone knew it was pointless to argue, so we just kept packing. I don't know how many trips we had to make to the moving store that day to buy yet more boxes, more tape and bubble wrap, but each trip took a little more out of me.

Twelve people packed and loaded for ten hours that day. For most of that time, my mother sat in the middle of the floor of her living room, breathing heavily, wrapping and packing only her watercolor paintings at a glacial pace while the rest of us sweated and panicked, throwing her belongings into boxes willy nilly, trying to keep up with the movers who were determined to empty the house.

94

Despite all the items she retrieved from the trash, the pile of refuse we left behind for the garbage men was impressive. When the moving van was all packed, one of the movers pulled my brother aside, as Clay had volunteered to drive the van from Wichita to Mom's new house in Topeka. "Don't go over 55 miles an hour," he advised. "It's not safe. That truck is way overweight and you need to leave yourself plenty of braking distance. And you definitely don't want to be stopped by the highway patrol." The rented moving van, which was just a tad smaller than a semi tractor-trailer and proclaimed in big letters on the side that it was *Perfect for moving a family of four!* was packed tight, bottom to top, back to front. We were all exhausted: hot, wet with sweat, muscles loose and rubber-bandish from the endless hauling, lifting and heaving.

As the sun began to get low in the sky and my brother pulled away in the big van, Mother said, "Well, that's almost all of it. We'll have to come back Monday for the rest." My brain screamed with fury but I kept my mouth clamped shut, because I knew if I opened it, things wouldn't end well. There were a few of her belongings left in the house, but it was the things in the yard, much of which I had assumed was staying, that Mother once again insisted could not be left behind. It was as if we were asking her to abandon kittens in the gutter. Tools, hoses, plastic chairs, sprinklers—those things I could understand taking. But it was the random yard junk and the 75 or so potted plants that I couldn't. And that's when I realized where most of her packing efforts had gone: taking starts from her garden plants and potting them so she could reboot her new-slash-old life in Topeka.

95

Jim drove our car back to Lawrence while I prepared to drive Mother in her car, a ridiculous gold Chrysler Fifth Avenue that her parents had given to her when they'd upgraded to an even larger Crown Victoria. After I'd beat the shit out of it dragging around town doing unscrupulous things as a senior in high school, my mother had further degraded the car by, in her words, "Treating it like a pickup truck." She'd used it to haul her gardening materials and salvage. Now it was packed to the hilt with more "treasures" my mother couldn't bear to part with, and when we arrived in Lawrence we would find that a rusty old can of paint had overturned in the back seat, forever staining it pink. She was too tired to drive, so I took the wheel. As we got underway, my mother snuggled herself into the passenger seat, preparing to nap. "Take me to get a shake at Hardee's," she said in baby talk. "I travel better with ice cream in me." I gritted my teeth, wanting to throttle her. I think she thought the baby talk made her vulnerable and endearing. It made me want to drive into a tree and murder us both. Nevertheless, I stopped on the turnpike to get her damn shake, which she sipped in silence before falling asleep.

Clay and I made the trip back to the Wichita house alone while Mother settled in to her new place in Topeka. I couldn't believe we were there again, with hours of work ahead of us in the hot sun, hauling things out of the yard and shoving them into the moving van. We marched back and forth in silence, carrying pot after pot. I began to feel sorry for myself. My eyes filled with tears. It was too much. We were only performing this absurd task because we were afraid of what Mother might do if we didn't. Of the shitstorm that might rain down on us were she

96

denied her crap. I was hot, tired, sweaty and sore. As we passed each other, Clay saw the look on my face. Suddenly, he barked out in time with his march: "MORALE IS LOW. WORKERS LOSING HOPE." Like most siblings, we have a strange sense of humor we share. Even in the midst of our most vicious fights as kids we could be beating the shit out of each other one second and laughing our heads off the next. Sometimes I think it was the only thing that kept us from going to the dark side.

We filled the floor of the moving van with as much stuff as we were willing to load. When we met Mom at her new place, she chastised us for the things we'd left behind. But we were finished, and we weren't going back.

In the aftermath of the move, Mother was not as much grateful for the help as she was irritated by the impreciseness of the packing, finding it difficult to locate the things she wanted. She was also annoyed by the number of things that were broken, which was in my opinion, negligible.

All of the hopes I'd had for Mother in her new house were pretty much dashed in the first year, and her move closer didn't improve our relationship. I made the mistake of thinking that I could take control of her life and direct it in such a way that we'd both be happier. This of course made her defensive and suspicious of me. At one point I expressed my disappointment that she hadn't taken better advantage of her new start and she bristled as though I'd slapped her. "What?" Did you expect me to be *instantly* well?" She spat these words in her best Betty Davis-esque voice.

Instantly? I thought, knowing at that point that Mom was lost to me and never coming back. She'd been assuring me for the last twenty years that she was on her way to getting better. It would just take the right therapist, the right bottle of supplements, the right medication. I came to the realization that there's nothing I can do for my mother. No clinic I can take her to, no doctor who will make her better. Because this is the United States of America. And in the United States of America, we are all free. Free to descend into the depths of madness and despair, with no one and no safety net to cradle our fall.

The effect of my mother's mental health has been to nibble away at my own, which I often struggle to hold on to, like runny eggs slipping through my fingers. But I know have to stay sane, because my daughter is depending on me. So I cup my hands tight around my runny eggs as I try to move forward and stay positive. Most days, I can hold on to them. Some days not.

Chicken Divan

I have always eaten with enthusiasm. For many years, from about the age of 3 until I was about 9, the dish I asked my mother to make for my birthdays was Chicken Divan. She made it for me without fail, lovingly and happily, and I would wolf up helping after helping until I was ready to burst. This recipe comes from one of those collected housewives' cookbooks from the Wichita community in, I think, the 1960s. (Apparently back then people subsisted almost entirely on mayonnaise, sour cream, bacon, Jello and cheese, because that's what most of these recipes seem to contain.)

Ingredients
1 large can (or two small cans) cream of chicken or cream of onion soup
1 cup mayonnaise
1 8 ounce container sour cream
1 tablespoon lemon juice
1 tablespoon curry powder
6 chicken breasts, poached until tender
2 12-ounce packages frozen broccoli florets
2 cups shredded cheddar cheese

Method: In a large bowl, combine soup, mayonnaise, milk, cheese, lemon juice, and curry to make sauce. Place shredded chicken and broccoli in large casserole dish. Pour sauce over all. Top with shredded cheese. Cover baking dish with foil. Bake at 350 degrees for 30 minutes, then remove foil and bake another 10 minutes.

Dad and the M-80

     My dad grew up in the "gee-whiz" days of the 1950s. I'm not making fun of that. I grew up in the "oh-mi-god!" days of the 1980s. To this day, Dad retains a lot of the *Leave it to Beaver-* and *Grease*-esque language and sense of mischief of his youth. So when he had a chance to buy a couple of "real" M-80s, the kind that are illegal in the United States, he jumped at it.

     He bought them from a friend who had supposedly acquired them in Germany and then smuggled them into the U.S. The purchase was thrilling for my dad for two reasons: 1) He had two *real* M-80s in his possession! 2) Dad is one of those people who drives around with a bumper-sticker on his car that proclaims **Gun control means hitting your target** so the idea of subverting the government with small explosives was pleasing to him. He had the firecrackers for several weeks and when he'd call me he'd mention them. "Sometime we've gotta go out and blow these bad-ass sons-a-bitches up!" he'd say, as though I was just as enthused about it as he was. "Yeah, Dad. We've got to do that sometime. Talk to you later." *Click.*

     But he was persistent and at some point, I could no longer put him off. The idea of going out into the country with

Dad to watch a couple of spilt-second explosions seemed pretty lame to me, and I brought the matter up to Jim, apologizing. "Look, I'm sorry, but Dad *really* wants us to go out with him and fire off these M-80s and he *really* wants *all* of us to come along." All of us being myself, Jim and my brother Clay. I could see Jim wondering yet again what kind of nut-job family he'd married into, but being that Jim also had the kind of dad who could be very insistent, he understood my predicament and agreed to go. We piled into Dad's van one fine summer evening and went forth to practice every American's god-given right to blow a big-ass hole into an object of our choosing. Because Dad was convinced that these M-80s were equivalent to a quarter stick of dynamite. *A quarter stick of dynamite!* he'd exclaim, eyes twinkling. He'd squint and point his finger for emphasis as if to say: *You can't even believe I have this kind of illegal explosive in my possession, can you? And that faggoty ass Bill Clinton can't do anything about it, because I am a goddamned patriot.*

My dad is a guy who's self-sufficient and likes to be prepared. For as long as I can remember he's carried a collapsible military surplus shovel in his vehicle which has come in handy to scoop a tire out of the snow or dig up a fetching patch of Kansas wildflowers. On this trip I noticed that Dad had added a military surplus gas can to his van. This was for two reasons, one so that he'd never find himself stranded without fuel and also he could stock up on cheap gas. I have seen my dad drive miles out of his way to save a single penny per gallon on gas. But the gas can was not sealed very well, because the three of us—Clay, Jim and I—looked at each other asking silently: *Do you smell that? Of course I smell that. How could you not smell that? How can Dad not smell that? It* reeks *of gasoline in here!* Which might account for my Dad's increased paranoia and ever more fervent political views, but who knows. Thank goodness the windows in the van were all down, because for many years, my dad refused to use the air conditioning in his vehicles insisting that it significantly reduced the number of miles per gallon of gasoline he could drive. Forever in my mind's eye will be the picture of my dad's tanned left arm hanging out of his minivan, now and again shoving a handful of sunflower seeds into his cheek and spitting the shells into the wind. Now that he's older and doesn't take the heat as well, he's relaxed his air conditioning ban, but he'll probably always eat sunflower seeds while he drives.

The four of us were under the impression that we could drive out into the county and find plenty of open space in which to blow something up. But we learned a lesson in urban sprawl that evening. We drove around on dusty dirt roads for a full hour-and-a-half just trying to find a spot secluded enough to make a loud bang without either scaring the crap out of someone or drawing some farmer out of his house with a shotgun a la Red Dawn. Finally, just as Dad was about to give up and drive us home, we found a deserted stretch of road.

Dad had brought along an old galvanized metal bucket that he'd intended to invert and set down over the first M-80, convinced that the bucket would be blown to smithereens. As he prepared to light the big firecracker, Clay, Jim and I took cover behind the van to avoid being hit by shrapnel. By this point, the three of us were fully invested in this outing. We'd wasted a good portion of our evening riding around like lunatics in a van with illegal explosives when we could've been relaxing in front of the television like normal Americans, so at this point, we were ready to be party to the hooliganism. Dad lit the M-80, dropped the bucket over it and we steeled ourselves for the *BOOM*. What happened next was like watching some sort of slow motion, acid-induced Looney Tunes episode come to life.

As soon as Dad lit the fuse he became a man running for his life. Only he didn't go anywhere. His feet bicycled in place, slipping and sliding on the gravel. The terror in his eyes couldn't have been more real if someone had held a loaded gun to his forehead.

After what seemed like several seconds, he fell. He got up. Being that it was summer in Kansas, he was wearing shorts. Hot blood flowed freely from his 60-year-old knees and ran down his legs. He began to run again. Again, his legs bicycled uselessly beneath him. His eyes were wild with fear and we were afraid with him, panicked that we'd have to drive him to the ER and explain how our sixty year old father had ended up with galvanized scrap material embedded in his keester. Somehow, at the very last second, he found enough traction to scuttle behind the van, cowering with us.

With a disappointing *POOF!* the M-80 blew the bucket about two feet off the ground, ripping open about three inches of the bucket's welded seam. And that was it. All of the driving and the sweating, the huffing of gas fumes and choking on country road dust for less than a split second of underwhelming banality.

"God dammit!" Dad swore, and I felt a little sorry for him. Clay and Jim did their best not to laugh.

In addition to the two bloody gouges in his knees, Dad showed us that in the fall, he'd managed to remove most of the

103

skin from one elbow. Then he walked away from us, put the bucket over the second M-80 and lit it. This time, he didn't bother to run. He sort of sauntered away. And we didn't bother to cower behind the van. We all stood out in the open to watch the second *pop*, which did a little more damage to the bucket, but not much. Then we drove back to town and Dad dropped us off at home without ceremony as we promised to get together again soon.

That night, it occurred to me that Dad's desire to blow up an M-80 was like any attempt that any of us make to recapture a fleeting spark of our youth, and usually, those attempts fall flat. Our bodies simply can't take it anymore. We can't run or drink or screw or dance or stay up all night like we used to. But we have to try once in awhile don't we? And we can't do it on our own. We have to rope someone else into the foolishness. And then we end up hung over and exhausted, with a kink in the neck or chafing in the groin, or even hot blood running down our knees.

Miss Ma'am

Like everyone else on planet Earth who's ever had a child, I'll never forget that moment when our only baby girl was born and placed on my chest. I've seen births on television where the mother immediately begins to coo and weep, clutching her newborn as if he or she were made of the very fabric of the universe, while the dad looks on in awe, as if he were Adam, staring at one of the first stars to appear in the sky.

That is not what happened when the doctor handed our daughter to me, my husband standing next to me, both of us breathless. The thickness of the thing that hung in that air was so palpable it could have been bottled:

Ho-ly shit. What the fuck have we done, and what the fuck do we do now?

Because I honestly don't think we'd thought about it that much. Up until that point, we'd been almost focused on my pregnancy and the birth. Once she physically existed in the world we were totally clueless as to what to do with her, and it was the singular most terrifying point in my life.

One would think that being a human being would mean that taking care of a human infant would be instinctual. No such luck. It was as if Jim and I had gone to the zoo and while we were there, one of the kookaburras had just given birth and a zookeeper had handed us the newborn kookaburra, saying, "Here. Take this kookaburra baby. Take her and name her and love her and keep her safe and make her one of your own." Without any instructions and barely any knowledge of what a kookaburra is. And maybe this hypothetical zookeeper had been kind enough to give us a single book titled, *What to Expect the First Year with Your New Kookaburra*, only the book turned out to be just as frightening and mysterious as the kookaburra itself, and in the end, almost completely worthless and full of shit, making you want to throw the book across the room, hopelessly sobbing along with your newborn kookaburra.

But of course, we named her and took her home and immediately began muddling through the process of keeping her from dying while I hardly slept, because I was thick in the throes of that all-consuming new-mother panic in which I was convinced that my sleep equaled her demise. This was the first time in our marriage that Jim and I fought. Up until that point, we'd enjoyed eleven years of mostly happy, low-stress togetherness. Now I was so tired I couldn't even make the simplest of decisions. I'd call Jim at work, sobbing because I couldn't decide whether to make tacos or spaghetti for dinner. I mean, the lettuce and tomatoes needed to be used up, but so did the ground turkey I'd bought to make the meatballs.

"It doesn't *matter*," he'd say, exasperated. "Just pick one!" Because he was just as tired as I was and he knew that whatever choice he made would be the wrong one, anyway.

The Geneva Convention has rules about sleep deprivation. Babies do not know about the Geneva Convention. In my resulting brain fog, I would sometimes be temporarily thrown into a minor panic, thinking that my Jim and I had altered our lives in such a way that our new 24-hour schedule was permanent, until the day we fell down dead. Then I'd remember that she wouldn't be a baby forever, she *had* to grow up, and I'd relax again. Mixed with those moments were the moments when I'd be holding her in my arms in the middle of night looking at her little face and find myself convinced that she was far wiser than me. That she could read my thoughts and see into my soul. I know it was just the lack of sleep distorting my brain, but that didn't make the moments any less mystical.

Speaking of her little face, I found that spending all day with her perfect, doll-like body, her head no bigger than a grapefruit, made Jim's head seem all that much more freakishly gigantic when he'd lie down next to me in bed at night. Speaking of large fruit, I'll never forget when my milk came in and my breasts swelled up to the size and firmness of two hard cantaloupes. Two big, disgusting white cantaloupes with bulging blue veins running over their surfaces. (These are the kinds of things that no one tells you before you get pregnant, because old ladies have an inherit interest in the continuation of the species.) At first, I looked at them and wanted to cry. Then, I held one of the cantaloupes up to the grapefruit and prayed that those little rosebud lips would take the pressure off my turgid bazongas. And they did.

Adding to the stress of the complete upheaval in our lives was the fact that starting when she was just a few weeks old, our baby was bored. Intellectually, I know that it's not possible for a six week old baby to be bored. But she *was*. She was fussy and colicky, and when I sat at home with her she whined and squeaked and cried almost non-stop, unless she was feeding or sleeping. "You'll get to know your babies cries," older people would insist. "You'll be able to tell her 'I'm wet' cry from her 'I'm hungry' cry," they'd say, but I couldn't tell the difference. Soon I began to feel as if my entire existence was dedicated to easing her discomfort, a round-the-clock task at which I failed day after day after day. Once, while visiting and watching his granddaughter fuss, Dad commented: "Can you imagine that? Not being able to communicate? You could be too hot or too cold or have an itch in the middle of your back … anything … and nobody would ever know." I was horrified.

After a few weeks, I took to putting her into a baby carrier while wandering aimlessly through stores. I couldn't buy anything because I'd quit my job to stay home with her. It didn't matter which store we went to, just as long as I didn't stop moving. Even though she was just a few weeks old and facing my chest, she had the strength to crane her little neck around so that her developing eyes and brain could take in all the colors, all the shapes. As soon as I'd take more than a few seconds to consider an item, she'd start squawking and fussing, so I'd move on to the next thing for her little mind to catalogue. As she grew, the fabric store was a great place to go, because of all the colors and textures of the fabric, which she loved to grab for.

Her disposition improved once she could sit up and grasp toys, but eventually she'd become frustrated and bored not being able to move from one spot. To this day, she's utterly kinetic and always fighting back tides of tedium.

Though some people are enamored of babies, I was thrilled when we could begin communicating with each other, which happened long before she could speak. When she didn't like the song playing on the radio while we were riding in the car, she'd shake her head vigorously, with her thumb planted in her mouth. "Mmmm, Mmmm," she'd say, until I'd tune in a song that was acceptable. Once, when we were tending to the cats at a friends' farm while they were out of town, Miss Ma'am, who was in my arms, pointed to a large propane tank and asked in toddler gibberish what it was.

I sighed, not knowing what to say, still feeling new-mommy tired. "Well ... " I said, hesitating, "It's complicated." Because I really wanted to tell her exactly what it was. I'd made a conscious decision after she was born that I would always do my best to tell her the truth, a luxury that was often not afforded to me when I was growing up.

She made a motion with her tiny arm, the way kids do when they're trying to get a trucker to honk his horn, and at the same time, emitted a high-pitched train whistle noise: "Wooo, woooo!"

"That's right," I said, nodding. "It's a train."

I started calling her "Miss Ma'am," because it fit her so well: Her one goal, focused like a laser beam since the moment of her birth, is to grow up. Jim's mother took to the nickname immediately, delighting in the title. "Miss Ma'am!" she'd say, watching her granddaughter toddle around her house, "What do you think you're doing, Miss Ma'am?"

When she was nearing the age of two, Miss Ma'am began to talk in earnest, twittering like a little bird from the second she'd open her eyes in the morning until the moment she collapsed into sleep at night. I'd give anything to hear that musical little voice chirping away again for just a few precious seconds, but at the time, there were days that by evening I was so overloaded by the incessant chittering I wanted to rip my own ears off. By the time she was two and a half we had to buy her a big-girl bed because one night, she simply refused to sleep in her crib, opting instead to sleep in the twin bed in the guest room. Six months later she was potty training and thank goodness her favorite movies at the time were *Mary Poppins* and *Harry Potter*, because each time she'd take her place on her tiny throne she'd declare with utmost certainty: "Mary Poppins goes potty on the pot." Or "Harry Potter goes potty on the pot." It was as if the word gods had bestowed me with the gift of my favorite literary device—alliteration—through my golden babe's own mouth.

And yes, we let her watch television, and even more horrible, we let her watch entire movies, which she did with earnest from a disturbingly young age, about three and a half. In our defense, we also read to her several times a day, played with her constantly, and her father began showing her flashcards and teaching her to write when she could barely hold a crayon. Putting on a movie was an hour-and-a-half respite for me during the day when I didn't have to interact with her, because she insisted I be within her sight at all times. I guess I assumed that she understood the plots of the movies from the time she began watching them because she did so with such interest, but that wasn't the case. A full year later, I watched the light bulb turn on when she realized that movies weren't just a succession of random scenes, but an entire story that progressed from beginning to end. At that point, we couldn't watch any movie without an endless stream of questions:

"Who's that? Where's she going? Why is she going there? Why did she stop? Why is she saying that? What's in her bag? Who's he? Is that her friend? Where did he come from? Why did he say that? Does she like him? Are they friends? What does he have in his hand? Is he sad? What is she thinking about? Why did that happen? *What's going to happen next?*"

About the time she started watching movies she began to ask why her feet didn't reach the bottom of the bed the way Daddy's and my feet did. She would also scooch to the very edge of the couch so that the tips of her toes would just brush the carpet. "Momma, wook … " she'd say, and I knew that she was indicating that her feet did not *have* to swing in the air when she sat on the couch, but could, in fact, reach the floor just like grownup feet.

It was the age of four or so when she developed a fascination with ancient Egypt, mummies, pyramids, skeletons, graveyards and tombstones. It was the same age that I watched her come into the understanding of the concept of death, which at first disturbed her very much. Soon, though, she seemed to grab onto the notion of death in order to try and take control of her fear. She began making construction paper tombstones that she'd affix to the carpet with masking tape so that they would stand up like real tombstones, then lie down in front of them. Death became a sort of game to her. In her play world, skeletons and mummies regularly emerged from their graves and tombs to mingle with the living. She transformed the undead to poor souls who were misunderstood. She would ask me to wrap her in ace bandages or toilet paper so that she could play "deceased Egyptian pharaoh," or sometimes she'd pretend to be a skeleton.

111

"Oh, hello there, little skeleton," I'd say with mock surprise.

"Hi," she'd say, giving a shy little wave.

"Where did you come from? Do you need a place to live?"

"Yes, please. I came from that cemetery over there. I don't know where my parents are."

"Well you may come and live with me and my husband, little skeleton. We'd love to have a little skeleton to take care of."

"Okay," she'd say happily. Then she'd shrug her shoulders. "We can just dig a grave for me in your back yard and I'll sleep out there!"

Once, she made a paper tombstone, wrote her name across it and asked me to take her picture while lying in front of it. I declined, telling her that I couldn't because it would make me too sad. (Not only that, but it would've provided photographic evidence of my fucked-up parenting.)

One summer morning when I was out of ideas to keep her entertained, we went with her "Aunt Winda" to Lawrence's historic Oak Hill Cemetery and made rubbings of the more interesting tombstones. We returned home hot and tired and thirsty, but Miss Ma'am was pleased with her rubbings, which she showed her father when he came home from work that day, and which stayed rolled up in her closet for six months or so until I snuck them into the trash.

In order to stay her boredom, she began authoring her own books, dictating the text to Jim or me and filling in the illustrations herself. She wrote plays and movie scripts and had me follow her around with the video camera. Even now, when she plays with friends, their parents will often smile at me and say, "We were treated to a play today," because Miss Ma'am manages to snare her friends into her productions.

To this day, she goes through reams of paper, yards and yards of tape, pounds of staples and bucketfuls of glue. She draws, paints, sculpts and builds. I began signing her up for art classes at our local Arts Center as soon as they would take her, at the age of three. I think that's where she got the idea to begin raiding our recycling bin for materials for her endless stream of projects. By the age of seven, she'd become the queen of the hot glue gun and Jim and I gave up worrying about her burning herself because it wasn't worth the endless arguments.

She fashions works of function and art from paper, coffee filters, disposable silverware, pieces of her toys, paper towel tubes, rubber bands, Kleenex boxes, string, paper clips, cereal boxes, tin cans, popsicle sticks, toothpicks, plastic bottles and just about anything she can get us to say "yes" to letting her have. She creates any number and variety of robots, spaceships, cars, models, buildings, musical instruments and even a Velveeta-box ship that's docked on Jim's dresser as of this writing. If she doesn't have a particular costume for a play or a game of pretend, she creates her own hats, swords, guns, moustaches and assorted accessories from cardboard, yarn and construction paper. One morning at the age of five she made Mario and Luigi caps out of red and green construction paper for her father and herself, without any help or instruction whatsoever. She just did it. She's made herself a pirate hat and eye patch, more than once. At the age of eight she could whip out a pair of chipboard- and duct tape flip-flops in under an hour, which she might choose to wear to a play date at the park.

That's not a joke.

To this day, she exhausts and bewilders me, almost as much as the day she was born. By the tender age of three she had already decided that she knows far more than either her father or I do, and as such, I dread with all my being the age of eleven, and then thirteen, and just the *thought* of sixteen and eighteen makes me want to set off smoke bombs and run away. Still, it's a *great* sense of exhaustion, the kind that you might feel blasting off in a rocket, embarking on a frightening trip to some strange, but wonderful, new world.

Miss Ma'am's Coffee

Miss Ma'am noticed very early on that I drink coffee every morning, and pretty much as soon as she could talk, she was demanding her own cup 'o' Joe to drink along with me. This is the recipe I came up with to keep her happy. Obviously, if you have ethical or moral objections to sucralose, you may substitute good old sugar.

Ingredients:
½ cup milk of your choosing
2 packets sucralose
2 or 3 drops vanilla extract

Method:
Mix all ingredients thoroughly in a child-proof cup. Serve to your child immediately, preferably while you're drinking your own coffee.

Santa, King of Lies

Growing up, one thing my parents never encouraged was telling the truth. In fact, they explicitly taught us kids that lying was perfectly acceptable when necessary to save one's ass. My mother once told my brother and me that were we ever called to the stand during one of the many court cases Dad instigated in his attempts to get equal custody of us, the two of us were to lie about whatever facts might cause a judge to decide to overturn her custody rights.

"I don't care if you've just put your right hand on a Bible and sworn to tell the truth, the whole truth and nothing but the truth. You *lie*." She said to us, more than once, and my mom is a God-fearing woman. But apparently, even more than her fear of God, Mom's biggest fear was that she'd lose us.

Dad was no less truthful. In fact, there were perpetually a whole pack of lies that my brother Clay and I were to maintain in the face of each parent on behalf of each parent. "Don't you *dare* tell your father we bought X …" or "Now, your mother really doesn't need to know that I sold this piece of glass." Since I was the oldest and the most verbal, most of the keeping track of the lies fell to me. Besides, Clay has never really had a disposition for lying. I, on the other hand, was quite good at it. Eventually, I considered myself to be somewhat of an expert at

116

lying, a skill that served me well during my teenage years. I learned that in order to be a good liar, one must develop a complete disregard for truthfulness. When you feel no guilt over it, lying becomes the easiest thing in the world. I got to the point that I could look right in my parents' faces, a teacher's face, a friend's parent's face, and tell a successful lie without feeling anything except a tingly sense of accomplishment.

When I left home and began to make my own way in the world, it started to dawn on me that maybe lying wasn't a skill of which to be proud. I also began to realize that the truth wasn't so horrible. The truth, I figured out over time, wasn't something to be feared. On the contrary, the more I practiced it, the more I found telling the truth to be quite freeing.

When our child, whom I'll call 'J,' was born, I made the conscious decision that I would tell her the truth whenever possible and always encourage her to do the same. At first, I wondered how, and if, I'd be able to do it. What would be the hurdles? The difficulties? In practice, I found it to be easy. I generally wait until she comes to me with questions, and then I offer only as much information as is appropriate given her age at the time. We've discussed things like stranger danger and death when Jim's parents died. In typical liberal fashion, we've talked with her about our stance on evolution and our support of families with two moms or two dads. When she began to have questions about God and religion, again, we were honest with her: We told J that we don't believe in God, but we acknowledge that most other people in the world do, and that she's perfectly within her rights to believe in God if she so chooses.

The sex question hasn't come up yet.

The one big lie that we have consistently told our daughter, the one that I kick myself every time I tell it, the lie that's like a tiny little knife stabbing me in the heart every time I hear myself repeating it, is that Santa Claus is real.

When she was about four years old J once said to me, "Mom, there are three people in the world who are magic, right?" Then she ticked them off her fingers: "Jesus, the Tooth Fairy and Santa Claus." (She'd learned about Jesus from various relatives and by attending vacation Bible school at the behest of one of her aunts.)

"That's right," I heard myself agreeing. "Jesus, the Tooth Fairy and Santa Claus are the only magic people in the world."

"And the Easter Bunny," she said. "But he's not really a *person*."

And it was *fine* for her to believe in Santa when she was four. We *wanted* her to believe in Santa when she was four. What more wondrous belief is there when you're little that you'll go to sleep at night and wake up in the morning to find a brightly wrapped gift that's just for you? A gift that Santa picked out for you specifically, out of the billions of kids all over the planet. *That is* magic. Now, though, it's just going on too long, but at this point I feel obligated to uphold the Santa lie because she's the one clinging to it like a Titanic victim to a life preserver. No matter how many times kids her age try to convince her that Santa isn't real, she isn't buying it.

"Mom," she sometimes asks, "is Santa real? Is he really real?"

My mind races. Do I keep up the lie? Or destroy her fragile psyche with the truth? "Of course Santa is real,

118

Sweetheart." I always say it, but I can't look her in the face when I do.

I can clearly remember when the Santa lie was shattered for me. I was in the second grade, and the topic of Santa came up in conversation. I'd probably said something to the effect that he'd really come through for me that Christmas.

"There is no Santa Claus, you know," one of the smart, cute boys in my class said. "It's just your parents."

"Yes he is," I said, bristling. The next thing I knew, I was surrounded by several seven- and eight-year-old Santa interventionists trying to talk me out of my delusion. My mind was temporarily blown up at the sheer number of non-believers in our class. How was it possible that so many children could've been lead so far astray? After a couple minutes of verbal wrangling, it hit me like a ton of bricks, right then and there: They were right. After all, which was more likely? That a magic fat man could travel all around the world in one night delivering presents to every single child on the planet? Or that the grownups living in your house, the ones who knew you best and had helped you write your wish list were the ones who filled the stockings and placed the gifts under the tree?

I keep waiting for my kid to become sensible and just drop the Santa thing on her own. She's now in the third grade, and though she's a good student, I can see her willfully holding on to the Santa fantasy despite all rational evidence to the contrary. Now, not only does she persist in the belief that Santa has the power to deliver anything one's heart desires, but she insists that Santa can deliver outdated technology—say for instance, an old video game system that's no longer in production. She is also *positive* that Santa could, if he wanted, deliver presents with magical properties, such as clothing that grows with you. He would probably even take back broken gifts for repair or exchange if one were to leave them out for him. When she makes these assertions, I feel my heartbeat quicken. *Where are we going to find an old Sega video game system for Christmas? Who makes adjustable shoes that grow with your feet?*

"Well ... Honey ..." I say, rubbing my temples and wondering exactly how long her father and I can let this deception go on, "I don't know if Santa really has time for all of *that*." And then I wonder: How can we tell her we're atheists on the one hand, but make her believe that *we* believe in the Pagan fat man who travels all around the world in a voodoo rig pulled by enchanted livestock on the other? *Exactly what kind of morally ambiguous people are we?*

"*Mom*," J says to me with pity. "He's *Santa*. He can do *anything*."

That he can.

Moving to Maryland

Every true Kansan will tell you that despite the lack of showy scenery such as mountains or oceans, we love it here and we mean it with all our hearts. The high plains are a sort of ocean of their own, a sea of land with its own unique rhythms and colors. It's not ostentatious beauty. It's a subtle, undulating grace that works its way into your psyche.

For the majority of our lives, Jim and I have loved the small city we live in, Lawrence, like an affair. She's cheeky and smart, gorgeous but comfortable. But in our early 40s we were beginning to feel as though Lawrence had let us down. We'd seen too many people become trapped in Lawrence, like bugs in a web, wanting to leave—in fact, many of them did leave—but they'd always return. And what did they come home to? A beautiful little college town with an educated populace, great restaurants and more artists than you can shake a stick at … but where few people make a great living. This fact, in the middle of our lives, was beginning to wear on both of us. Jim had grown tired of his job and the two-hour commute into Kansas City, Missouri every day. I worried about him in rush hour traffic. I'd watched my chosen profession—journalism—continue to do nothing but shrink, especially in the Midwest.

In the summer of 2011, I indulged in that selfish pity party known as the midlife crisis. I moped around, hating everything and blaming all my unhappiness on outside forces. Jim found me one night, crying in front of the television. "Don't you love me at all?" he asked.

"It's not you," I sobbed. "It's this place. We're so … stuck." And that was how it felt. As though we were stuck professionally, and literally, in the middle of the United States. Though Kansas is a lovely place, the weather is often uncomfortable—too hot, too cold, too dry, too windy, too tornado-ey—and the things that are worth visiting here are sometimes few and far between. To leave Kansas means hours of monotony in a vehicle or lots of money spent on plane tickets. Though Kansas summers are almost always hot and miserable, and the northeast corner of the state is humid to boot, the two previous summers had been off-the-charts unbearable. The heat had risen above 100 degrees every day for three months solid. Our family is so pale and sweaty that when the weather's like that we have no choice but to live like moles, rotting in front of a television or computer screen and scurrying from one air-conditioned building and vehicle to the next. Miss Ma'am and I had been to every local museum, every store and indoor kids' venue so many times we were both sick to death of all of them. For my family, to go swimming in the middle of the day in the middle of summer in Kansas is like boiling a slug with a magnifying glass.

Jim and I began to entertain the notion of cheating on Lawrence. Of leaving her. Leaving her for someplace with more opportunities and more things to do. Someplace with a landscape different than the one we'd been accustomed to our entire lives. For the first time we began to buy into the ignorance that people who don't live here try to impose on this place. Maybe Kansas *was* just flat and boring, with nothing to offer. Maybe a different outlook was what we needed. We began to have illicit thoughts about making a change that would pull us out of our midlife doldrums and put us on a path to happiness. (Insert yellow brick road allegory here.) On a lark, late that same summer, Jim applied for a job in Maryland that appealed to him. We were shocked when, a couple of weeks later, the company phoned him for an interview.

At that point, we didn't know what it might mean, so we kept it to ourselves. What we did was research Maryland like fiends, on everything from climate, to population, to things to do. We began to discuss the possibilities ... We'd be two hours from Washington D.C. and two-and-a-half hours from Baltimore. Four hours to the Atlantic Ocean. Six hours from *motherfucking New York City*. If Lawrence was a tiny cultural blue diamond in the middle of politically red Kansas, then moving to the Northeast could only mean *more* of the things we loved about our life in Lawrence, right? The museums! The theaters! The aquariums! The concerts! The restaurants! The excitement!

When Jim accepted the job, we told our family and friends and everyone was shocked. I'd like to say that they wished us well, but the truth of the matter is that I think most of them didn't—not that they wanted bad things for us, of course, but they didn't want us to go and couldn't understand why we were leaving. Mother asked if she could phone weekly and I said she could, giddy but guilt-ridden with the idea that she'd be halfway across the country instead of 30 minutes down the road. "Well *I* support you, in whatever decision you need to make for your family," Dad said. "But I *hate* the fucking east coast." This seemed like a great endorsement.

In all our research, we were surprised to find that like Kansas, Maryland is also known as the Free State. *The other Free State*, I thought to myself, and it seemed like fate.

It soon became apparent that we wouldn't be able to afford to live in the city in which Jim was employed, at least not in the sort of suburban digs we were used to. So we enlisted the help of a realtor, Addie, who compiled a list of potential houses in various towns near Jim's job. With her help, the internet and a quick trip out to the east coast, we managed to narrow the choice down to a couple of houses. We had also decided to delve into our savings and spend a few extra tens of thousands of dollars on a house because we had no idea what our new community would be like. We hoped that extra money would mean extra safety and good schools—all the things that uptight suburbanites of any race hope for, but perhaps not so fervently as middle class white people.

While we were mulling the house purchase, our realtor phoned to let us know that someone had put an offer in on one of the two houses we were considering, and it was the house I liked best. We made a counteroffer and within hours, we were the proud new owners of a home in Maryland. In another happenstance that seemed to reaffirm that the universe was rooting for our move, our friend Chuck, who had recently come into a boatload of cash after a smart business deal, offered to buy our Kansas house as an investment. It saved us from having to figure out how to pay two mortgages while J and I stayed behind trying to sell our old house in a down market. The upside of the down market was that home prices had fallen by almost half on the East Coast so we were able to obtain our new house for a steal, with one caveat: one of the owners had been out of work for over a year, so the couple insisted we pay the closing costs. This was something we'd never encountered before. In our part of the country, it's pretty customary for buyer and seller to split closing costs and closing costs are significantly higher in Maryland than in Kansas.

I appealed to Jim's conscience. "We've been lucky that we've pretty much gone untouched in this most recent recession," I reasoned. I reminded him that while his job had taken a hit when the tech bubble had burst in the 1990s, his salary had actually continued to go up during this latest recession. Plus, we'd made a nice profit on our previous house, selling it at the height of the housing bubble. I figured we could afford to take a little hit on the closing costs on this house and help out some fellow Americans who were down on their luck.

It was the purchase of the house that made the move solidify for all of us, and J began having panic attacks. *She'll be fine*, I told myself, though the anxiety that had begun to gnaw at *me* felt like more than butterflies. That night, after we'd tucked J in while she fretted about the move, I made for the stairs to feed the cat. In my head and unaware of what my feet were doing, I missed the last step of our staircase. It was something I'd done a dozen times before, always telling myself that next time, I might break something. As I fell hard on the landing, there was an audible "snap." The diagnosis at the ER was a broken fifth metatarsal, one of the long bones in my right foot.

Late that night, lying on my back with pillows piled around my temporary cast to keep my foot lolling to one side, I couldn't sleep. I squirmed, sweaty and uncomfortable despite the narcotics they'd prescribed me. My foot throbbed. If I'd worried before about how in the world we were going to get our entire house packed up and move across the country, now I was doubly so.

Monday morning I was able to see an orthopedist who took a look at the x-ray of my foot and declared, "That'll be healed in four weeks." *Four weeks?* I thought. *I'm forty.* It didn't sound right to me, but he was a respected doctor in the community so I took his word for it.

Jim took care of me while he worked his new job from home, getting me food, beverages, medication—everything, since it was impossible for me to carry anything while using crutches. He bought a plastic shower seat over his lunch hour one afternoon and helped me in and out of the shower every other day. He also got up every morning to get J ready for school and in the evenings, he began to pack up the house. I tried to sit and pack while wearing my new orthopedic boot, but after a couple of hours my foot would swell so much it'd feel like it was going to explode.

Ambulating with my new crutches was difficult. I've never had any upper body strength to speak of, so relying on my arms to haul my body weight was tiring and I was groggy from the pain killers. When I wanted to leave the house, I had to scoot down the stairs on my butt. Coming home, I had push myself back up the stairs on my backside, with my good foot.

After a week, I went back to the orthopedist. The new x-ray showed no improvement. He squinted at me. "Are you taking your supplements?" he asked. He also told me I needed to get rid of the crutches and start walking on my broken foot. "It'll hurt like hell," he said, "but you need to do it. The stress will help it heal." After that, I began placing my boot on the floor as I walked, but I still used the crutches. I couldn't give them up. The thought of putting all of my weight on a broken bone was too horrible.

In a couple of weeks we dubbed our new roommate "The stank foot." It was this useless, heavy object at the end of my leg that dictated what we did and didn't do and we all began to resent it, though Jim was sweet and supportive. The inside of an orthopedic boot is well-padded with foam and because I perspire heavily, it was soaking wet, all the time. I tried to make sure no one was near when I had to take it off because the smell was like that of sun-ripened cheese. The outside of the boot quickly became coated in dust and pet hair.

Over the next four weeks we scrambled to pack up the house. After the moving crew left with our things, I decided I was sick of sitting on my ass all the time. *Piss on it,* I thought. *I'm walking.*

Only I couldn't. In just four weeks, my leg muscles had atrophied so much that I had to grab at the walls to help myself along. My friend Jamie loaned me the cane she'd used after breaking an ankle so that I could hobble around. I hated, *detested* the boot. Even though it only weighed a couple of pounds, it felt like ten. The foot continued to swell until it was the size of a football every night. I took copious amounts of ibuprofen and naproxen sodium, both for the pain and with the hope that they would relieve the infernal swelling. The piling of the pillows at night became a ritual, both to relieve the swelling as well as to keep the big boot from pulling to one side or another, so Jim usually slept in another room, leaving me alone with my mountain of pillows.

Because I'd broken a bone in my right foot, I couldn't drive. So Jim drove us on the two-day trip to Maryland in one of our little Toyotas with our cat, Max. We drugged Max to try to keep him calm and stuffed him into a cat crate, and the first day he did okay. He wailed, but at least he was calm. The next day Max tried to scratch his way out of his crate until his claws bled, so we let him out. He weaseled around the car until he wedged himself under the passenger seat and disappeared.

I entertained myself on the trip making fun of Missouri on Facebook with my friends. As we traveled, the landscape became increasingly alien. Still, I was excited. *We're really doing it!* I thought. *We're getting out! We're going to be ex-Kansans!*

We spent the first night camping in our strange new home on the cold living room floor on air mattresses. None of us slept well, and Max wandered the empty house, yowling now and again in the night. We were roused by the movers who arrived with our belongings at precisely 7 a.m.

The house Jim had picked out was gorgeous. It was 400 square feet larger than our Kansas house, with wood floors throughout. The master bath had two sinks, a huge walk-in closet and a large soaking tub, luxuries we hadn't ever had before. The kitchen area was open and inviting, not cut off from the rest of the house like our old kitchen. And not only did the kitchen have space for a breakfast table but there was a separate formal dining and parlor area that was so spacious we didn't have close to enough furniture to fill it. We were living large. The house was perfect for parties, but of course we didn't know anyone, and as much as I wanted to invite my friends over to see, they were two thousand miles away.

A couple of days after arriving at our new house, Nancy and David arrived with our other car and our dog Rocky. Rocky is a good guard dog. He likes to bark at any passing person, cat, dog, rabbit or plastic bag that might blow by. We soon learned that the entire neighborhood was accustomed to cutting through our back yard in order to get to the grocery store just a block away, or to the bus stop where the teenagers waited to go to high school. This meant that Rocky started barking about 7 a.m. and continued to bark at random times throughout the day until we closed the blinds at night. We never knew when we might glance out the kitchen or living room windows to see a stranger stomping through our back yard. It kind of bothered us, and Jim was ready to put up a fence, but I didn't think it wise to make waves in our new neighborhood.

As we began to explore our new town, we were dismayed to find that it was mall-centered, and like so many malls in America, the main mall-proper looked as though it had seen its heyday sometime back in the 1980s. What remained was a functional, but depressing place where teenagers refused to gather on weekends. The rest of town seemed to be pretty proud of its chain stores and chain restaurants, boxes of fake beige stucco stacked together in strip malls. The town itself was a trucking hub, which meant that semis constantly barged through. Still, we tried to stay positive. Most of America lives the chain-store mall life. We'd just need to get used to it.

After two weeks, Jim was hit hard with strep throat, necessitating a trip to the urgent care clinic. He stayed home from work for two days, dozing in bed, and went back to work even though he should've spent the week at home. The following week, J was sick, and the week after that, I was. Around the same time that Jim fell ill, my laptop became so locked up with a virus it was rendered useless. What with the move, his new job and the strep, Jim was so tired when he wasn't working he didn't get around to debugging it for an entire week, leaving me high and dry, a junky without her fix.

I thought it strange when I tried to set up an appointment with a local orthopedist and his office staff seemed hesitant to talk to me. They asked for my information and said they'd call back. When a receptionist returned my call she said, *He's agreed to see you*, which I thought was odd. What did she mean he *agreed* to see me? I had a broken foot. He was an orthopedist who specialized in feet and was compatible with our insurance company. So what the hell was the issue?

I would soon learn finding a doctor in our new town was a whole different proposition than our old one. We were used to being able to see a new doctor in a matter of a week or two or sometimes, if matters were pressing, in the same day. But in our new town there were only two paths to becoming a new patient: visit the urgent care clinic and get a referral or spend a day making calls to find a physician who accepted your insurance and was taking new patients and then schedule an appointment two or three months in the future. Though I supposed the people who lived there were used to such things, it added to my general feeling of unease. When I related this information to Jim, at first he thought I was kidding.

I dressed in a blouse and jeans and even put on makeup the morning I went to see my new orthopedist. I ceremoniously removed the stank boot and attempted to put on a pair of shoes, since my previous orthopedist had assured me the foot would be completely healed by the six-week mark, and the visit to an orthopedist in Maryland would be nothing more than a technicality. I tried on two or three different pairs of shoes before finding a pair that didn't hurt too much. I wasn't concerned about the pain—I figured it was a remnant of the boot and would work itself out in a few days. But I dropped the stank boot into a tote bag and took it along to the appointment, just in case. When I met the Maryland orthopedist, I liked him immediately. He was talkative, good-natured and knowledgeable. We chitchatted for a bit. He asked me where I was from.

"Kansas," I said.

"Kansas?" His head whipped around as though I'd said I'd run away from the dumbass circus. The look on his face went from congenial to amused pity. He chuckled. Not with me, but *at* me. "Well, you're not in Kansas anymore, Dorothy. This is the big time," he turned back to his computer screen. "Kansas," he said again. He shook his head.

I sat on the medical table, blood boiling. *"Really?"* I screamed inside my head. *You think this place is the 'big time'? I am from Lawrence, Kansas, buster. The home of the University of Kansas. What world-class research or art or music has this shitty little berg turned out? Are there any authentic Jordanian or South American restaurants here? Nope. Just the goddamn Pizzeria Uno.* But I managed to keep my face neutral as he loaded my x-ray onto his iPad.

The next thing he told me made go from pissed-off to wanting to burst into tears, but somehow, I managed to hold that in too.

"Yeah … looking at this x-ray … basically … your foot hasn't healed at all. See here?" He handed me the iPad and sure enough, any idiot could see the wide black crack against the white of the bone. His words hit like a brick to the head. *Hasn't healed. At all.* What had been the point of clomping around in the stank boot for six weeks?

"Those shoes you're wearing aren't supporting your foot, so we'll just get you an orthopedic boot …" he turned to his nurse.

I grabbed for my tote bag. "I have an orthopedic boot," I said, realizing that since he thought I was from Hickville, U.S.A., he also assumed we had no modern medicine. I produced the despised stank boot. "I've been wearing this. I've worn it for six weeks solid, twenty-four hours a day. I haven't taken it off until this morning."

"Oh!" he said, surprised. "Well that looks perfectly acceptable." He took my shoe off, put the boot on my foot and proceeded to work the air pump on the boot until the pressure was painful.

He told me to come back in a month.

The Maryland orthopedist told me I didn't have to wear the boot at night, which was a huge relief. Wearing an orthopedic boot sort of like strapping your foot to a board, and I as I reached the seventh and eighth week in the boot, all those muscles that weren't able to articulate during the day began to rebel at night. The foot would wake me in the middle of the night, twitching and clenching and unclenching of its own accord.

This was about the time J quit sleeping in her room. Each night at bedtime she'd go into a full blown panic attack. Jim began sleeping in the guest room, while J and I slept in the big bed. As she fretted and thrashed around, our bedtime conversations went something like this:

"What if I'm bleeding?"

"Bleeding from where?"

"I don't know. What if I have a cut somewhere I don't know about? What if I bleed out?"

"Where did you learn the term 'bleed out?'"

"*Mythbusters.*"

"You don't have a cut anywhere."

"Are you sure?"

"I'm sure."

"How do you know?"

"Because I know. You don't have a cut."

"Are you sure you know I don't have a cut? I'm going to the bathroom and check."

These conversations would go on and on, way past her bedtime of 8:30 p.m., until I'd talk her down and lull her to sleep by telling her a story.

Jim and I watched as our confident, outgoing child who makes friends as easy as breathing completely unraveled. I've signed her up for countless summer classes in Lawrence, classes where she didn't know a single kid and she'd always walked into those situations with nothing more than a "'bye mom." By the completion of the class she'd be pissed that she'd made friends she might never see again. But something about Maryland knocked the wind out of her sails. It was devastating to see her go into her new school after Christmas break full of so much hope to crumble within a couple of weeks. She wasn't making friends and by the end of our first month in Maryland her vague worries had developed into a full-blown obsessive-compulsive disorder. She became convinced she'd been poisoned—or possibly poisoned—twenty, maybe fifty times a day. Being that it was winter, she was sure every outdoor surface was contaminated with ice melt that maybe she'd touched and then maybe her hand had slipped to her mouth and therefore she was poisoned with ice melt and could die at any moment. Because no matter how many times we tried to reassure her a little rock salt wasn't dangerous, she wasn't buying it. Or maybe the random half-dead weed she'd touched was poisonous and *that* would kill her at any moment. Or maybe the people who'd lived in the house before us had fitted the shower head in her bathroom with some sort of secret deadly gas dispenser and some morning she'd fall over dead in the shower.

The final straw was the night I tried to comfort my hysterical child with a hug and she shoved me away screaming,

"Don't touch me!" because she didn't want to infect me with whatever poisons she might have picked up that day. I spent the next day on the phone trying to find a counselor for her. After a couple of days, a psychologist returned my calls. She seemed friendly and competent and she agreed to work J into her schedule in the next few days.

"One thing," she said. "My office is in my church."

Ugh. I thought. I've never been a big fan of religion and certainly not religion and counseling in the same mix. Still, my kid was in trouble and this woman might be the only person who could help us, so I had no choice but to press forward.

"Do you practice a religious-based therapy?" I asked. My brain scrambled to choose the right words. Of course, I chose poorly. "Because my husband and I are atheists." *Why couldn't I just have said we weren't church goers?* I thought later.

The woman seemed taken aback. "Well … I don't *have* to talk with her about God when I counsel her," she said.

"It's okay if she wants to," I said. "It's up to her. If that's what makes her feel better then we don't mind."

I started volunteering to help out in J's classroom, hoping my presence would bring her some comfort. In order to get to the school, I had to stump out to the garage wearing the stank boot, sit down in the car, change out of the stank boot and into a slip-on shoe, and drive the mile or so down the road hoping I wouldn't have to stomp on the brake. In the school parking lot I'd change out of the shoe and back into the stank boot, stump up to the school where they'd buzz me in after showing ID and then up to J's second-floor classroom, all to the pitied looks of the teachers and volunteers I met on the way. Most days I started out feeling as if I'd rather stay home to write or fold laundry, but as it turned out, I had a good time working with the kids. They were bright and chatty, and rather than giving us crap about being from Kansas, they were intrigued.

"Mrs. Fraley, Mrs. Fraley, Mrs. Fraley! Aren't there *twisters* in Kansas?"

"Yes," I'd tell them. "There are lots of twisters."

Their eyes would widen.

"Have you ever seen one?" they'd ask.

"Nope," I'd say, shaking my head. "Never have. Though I hope to someday."

"I wouldn't want to," they'd say. "I don't *ever* want to be in a twister!"

They seemed sweet, and I couldn't understand why J was having such a tough time connecting with them.

"The girls are mean," she told me. But they didn't seem mean while I was there. So I'd argue with her, frustrated she wasn't fitting in, as if it was her fault. "That's not true. They're very nice. They *want* to be friends with you. You just have to give them a chance."

After a few weeks, though, I started to figure out what she was talking about. There was a fairly large clique of girls in the class, and my daughter wasn't in it. The clique was lead, as most girl cliques are, by one girl in particular, Chase. I noticed Chase wore designer clothes from the mall that outclassed the typical grade school wardrobes assembled from hand-me-downs, Target and Wal-Mart. If she didn't like you, and you were a girl, you lingered in a sort of social limbo. Sometimes Chase would throw J a social bone, but more often she treated

136

her as a mild annoyance, so the other girls in the clique, which amounted to about half the girls in the class, followed suit. Chase was endlessly polite and charming to me, and I was always kind to her, hoping somehow she would funnel some kindness back to my daughter.

I had expected my kid to come up against this kind of social bullshit when she reached middle school. It hadn't occurred to me that kids becoming douchebags had accelerated along with technology and everything else. I'm not saying there wasn't bullying at J's grade school in Kansas, it just hadn't happened to her. It's horrible to watch your kid be bullied, even a little bit, and girl bullying is difficult to prove because it often involves shunning. What I wanted to do was shake the shit out of every one of those little snots and tell them in no uncertain terms to quit fucking with my kid. Instead I smiled and kept my temper while reminding them to stay on task.

One of my favorite kids in J's class was a boy named Noah. Noah was a farm kid with a serious case of dyslexia, so I got to work with him a lot. He was sweet and polite and when I asked him what he was interested in, he said, "My animals." Whereas most boys would say Star Wars or Pokémon. Noah was often grubby and covered in small cuts and bruises. It was both fascinating and heartbreaking to watch him struggle through simple vocabulary word flashcards. Once, while concentrating on a word, his mouth opening and closing while no sound would come out, he looked at me and said, "I know the word but I can't say it." I have no doubt this was exactly what was happening to him. He was not a dumb child in any sense of the word. He just had a short somewhere between his brain and his mouth. Noah had a quiet sort of dignity about him. Rather than

137

become frustrated or angry, he tried his best and accepted the outcome. I admired his strength. I couldn't imagine what it would be like to be forced to go to school and fail, day after day after day.

One girl who was the subject of much talk and fascination for the kids was Madeline. Maddy's family were Jehovas Witness, and none of the other kids could wrap their heads around the fact that Maddy was not allowed to celebrate Christmas or even her own birthday.

"You don't get any presents for your birthday? Not ever?"

Maddy was a stout, resilient girl. She'd shrug her shoulders. "I get toys at other times during the year. You get used to it."

Bastardizing the name of Maddy's religion, the kids had decided that a mean god named Jehobo was the one preventing her from having cake and presents on her birthday and a tree and gifts for Christmas.

"I'm glad my family doesn't listen to Jehobo," they'd declare. "Jehobo is mean."

Driving past the high school my daughter would attend one day, I was dismayed to learn from the sign out front that the high school's mascot was the "Rebels." The thought that my daughter, a natural born Jayhawk, might one day be a "rebel" chewed at my heartstrings like a tick on a dog's balls. One day, having driven past the sign and once again been faced with the "rebel problem," it dawned on me I could simply choose to rebrand them as the Rebel Force from the Star Wars franchise. It was an epiphany that lifted a huge weight from my shoulders.

The first really warm spring evening several of the neighbors lingered in the cul-de-sac chatting, while the kids rode their bikes and scooters. I ventured out, hoping to meet some of them. Helen, a black woman in her 40s and Martha, a grey haired white lady in her late 50s immediately let me in on the cul-de-sac gossip. Since our neighborhood was technically out in the county, we didn't have city trash service, meaning we all subscribed to private trash pickup services. "John over there sneaks his trash into all the neighbors' trash cans in the middle of the night," Martha told me as Helen nodded sagely. They also pointed out the house down the street where an older couple lived with their mentally ill adult son. "He's not too much trouble because he's usually pretty drugged up," said Helen, "but you do want to keep an eye on him around the neighborhood kids," she said. "He's wandered out of the house without clothes on."

A man with a long gray ponytail and a skeevy mustache made his way toward us. He grabbed my hand, leaned over and kissed it. "*Enchanté*, Madame."

Martha rolled her eyes. "That's my husband Mike. Just ignore him."

In our misguided Midwestern naïveté, we had honestly thought Maryland was part of "The East Coast." A place we imagined to be replete with book reading, horn-rimmed glasses wearing, jazz listening, progressive-minded Americans. But I swear to God the only place I've seen more camouflage clothing than the part of Western Maryland we moved to is Branson, Missouri. It was on men, women and children. Camo t-shirts, camo sweat

139

shirts, camo pants, shorts, ball caps, boots and jackets. We saw pickup trucks wrapped in camo. And I couldn't figure out exactly what they were camouflaging themselves from. It would've made more sense if people had been wearing concrete gray or maybe fake stucco urban tan-colored clothing to blend in with all the Panera Breads and the Beds Baths and Beyonds. We were in the middle of a metro area, as far as I could tell, with humanity shoulder to shoulder, cars bumper to bumper and pavement as far as the eye could see. There was an enormous outlet mall just a mile down the road from us that brought in shoppers from four states. But one little boy in J's class told me the previous fall, his uncle had shot a twelve-point buck in the empty lot next to the Waffle House and my new neighbor Mike assured me that because of the smell of dung in the air, this was indeed a "rural area." It was considered a "rural area" because the farms and cows had to go somewhere and we were definitely living near several of them. But right next to the farms were grocery stores and strip malls. We have all that in Kansas, too, but these are called "cities." A "rural area" in Kansas is when your neighbor is the next farm five miles down the dirt road.

Because it was close by, we often found ourselves eating at the Cracker Barrel down the road, which was fine with my husband and daughter because as the name implies, the Cracker Barrel serves their favorite kind of cooking: white people food. Every time I hear the name "Cracker Barrel" I can't help but but wonder why they didn't go the extra step and name the place something like "Honkey Hut." I came to hate the Cracker Barrel with its dark, depressing interior and its reheated fatty food, but it was convenient and it made my family happy, so I didn't say anything.

One Sunday afternoon we decided to venture out to learn more about the area we'd moved to. We visited the Antietam battlefield and later a small nearby town with a rustic ice cream parlor that served gigantic ice cream cones. We returned home that evening tired, happy and ready for supper, only to discover that we were locked out of our house. Still not sure what the crime might be like in the area, Jim had insisted that the door in the garage that lead into the house be locked at all times. Trouble was, the key for that door was on my key ring, which was inside the house. The sun began to go down. It started to get cold. We sat in the car in the garage, Googling locksmiths on our smart phones, calling and getting nothing but answering machines. Eventually, J and I had to pee, so Jim drove us to the neighborhood grocery store. Desperate, I asked the woman at the service counter if she had any ideas about a locksmith that might work Sunday evenings. "This guy gave us his business card," she said, and handed it to me. I called and he said he'd be out right away.

It took an hour of finagling, but the door gave way unexpectedly and the guy landed flat on his face on our kitchen floor.

The one advantage to wearing an orthopedic boot is that one is given preferential treatment by pretty much everyone, everywhere. Parents standing twenty feet away would grab at their small children, pulling them close. "Watch out!" they'd say, pointing. "She has a broken leg! Don't trip over it!" For the first time in my life people got the hell out of my way and doors were held open for me everywhere. Old women tsk-tsked giving me looks of compassion. On the trip we took to the big aquarium in Baltimore, we first tried having Jim push me through in a wheelchair, but discovered that while public places may be *technically* handicapped accessible, it is annoying as shit to try to maneuver through crowds in a wheelchair in real life. So we gave the wheelchair back and I spent the rest of the visit swinging through the place on crutches, because by now, I was a crutches expert. "You are so brave," one woman said, making me feel like a total asshole. *Brave* is a word that should be reserved for those who go into combat or pull drowning children from burning buildings.

One thing that I found pleasant about Maryland was the birdsong floating on the air. I like to open the windows whenever possible and the never-ending twitter and chitter of birds from daybreak to sundown was soothing and happy. One never needed to put on music because it wasn't really necessary. The sound confounded me though, because it seemed so foreign. We had birds in Kansas. I was sure of it. I'd seen them. We'd fed them. So why didn't I remember *hearing* them? Hadn't there been the same noise there?

"Why don't you come back to my office where we can talk," J's therapist said to me after one of their sessions. "I've asked her if it's okay to discuss a few things with you and she's agreed." I was eager to hear what kind of progress J had made. She seemed to be getting along better. Though she still didn't have any close friends at school, she'd made a very good friend in the cul-de-sac, Helen's daughter Necia.

As we readied to leave, the therapist left me with this parting thought: "J has indicated that she might like to go to church, and I think it might help her. It's something you might consider."

On the drive home, I started to cry. "If you want to go to church, I'll take you myself," I said. "Daddy and I won't mind."

J seemed less sure about church than the therapist had indicated. She told me that the therapist had suggested that maybe J try *her* church. "She says the people at her church are nice, but the whole thing kind of freaks me out. I don't know what to do. I don't know if I want to go to church."

Even the shortest of outings in the car made us feel as though we were taking our lives into our hands. There was a two-lane north-south highway that ran in front of our housing division and connected several small towns for several miles (they called it a 'pike') and during rush hour traffic was heavy and fast. When we needed to leave our neighborhood we were forced out on the pike, usually by way of making a left turn, since that way led into town, while a right turn led down the road to the next town.

One Friday night we decided to go out to dinner not at the Cracker Barrel, but at the Longhorn Steakhouse, just a couple of miles down the pike. We were driving along at about 45 miles an hour in rush-hour traffic when a white wall appeared in front of us. Turned out the "wall" was a sedan driven by a teenage girl who'd somehow not seen our car and had turned left in front of us. Jim slammed on the breaks, but there was no room to decelerate. We t-boned her car, hard, going from a decent clip to a dead stop. Our windshield was spider-webbed with cracks and smoke billowed from the dash board. *We have to get out*, I thought. I was certain that either the car would blow up or more likely, someone else would hit us because we were sitting still in the middle of the pike. I grabbed J and traffic waited while I shuttled her to the side of the road. Jim reassured me that the car wasn't on fire; the smoke was caused by the firing of the airbags. I was amazed at the number of people who slowed down in the frantic rush of Friday night traffic and even stopped to ask if we were okay. One man made sure to pull over and tell the cop who detailed the accident that the teenage girl had flipped him the bird before cutting us off.

"I'm so sorry," the girl said to us, shaking. "I'm so sorry."

Our car was totaled. Because we still didn't know anyone well enough to have their phone number, there was no one to call to give us a ride home. Jim and J managed to catch a ride with the tow truck driver, while the cop reluctantly gave me a ride back to the house. The cop had gleaned from Jim's paperwork that we were from Kansas. "So you're Jayhawks," he said, smiling. "I'd love to move to Iowa," he said. "I love to hunt. I like the wide open spaces. I don't really like all the people out here, but I just can't seem to get away."

Though Jim's car was fully covered, he had put thousands of miles on it commuting back and forth to Kansas City and it was several years old. So the insurance company reimbursed us a whole seven thousand dollars. Not wanting to fool around with buying a used car, we dipped into our ever-dwindling savings and bought a new one. We had to come up with ten thousand dollars to make up the difference.

One by one, J's apocalyptic fears subsided until she was left with one single emotional tic. Every night, as we put her to bed in her own room, she'd ask, "Will anything bad happen tonight?" And though she didn't elaborate, I interpreted the subtext to be: "Will anyone break into the house in the middle of night, beat the shit out of us and take all our stuff?"

"No, Honey," I'd say. I'd kiss her on the cheek, hug her goodnight and think, *Jesus I hope not*.

Every year in Lawrence is a large Saint Patrick's Day Parade. Unlike some cities that insist on holding the parade on the Saturday nearest the holiday, Lawrence's Saint Patrick's Day Parade is always held on the day proper. That March, the holiday happened to fall on a Saturday, and it was Lawrence's largest Saint Patrick's Day Parade in the history of the event. Our Facebook feeds were full of our Lawrence friend's snapshots of their happy faces and goofy green hats and clothes.

Our new town let the day go by unnoticed.

March, of course, meant March Madness. In Lawrence, home of the University of Kansas Men's Basketball team, March Madness is a big deal. Nowhere in Maryland is March Madness a big deal, even when the Terrapins do happen to make it to the NCAA tournament. Like Saint Patrick's Day, we watched remotely as March Madness completely took over Lawrence. With every successive win, more and more people gathered

145

downtown after the games wearing their crimson and blue, drinking, high-fiving, fist-bumping and just generally having a kick-ass time. By the time the Final Four rolled around, downtown Lawrence was one big party, people shoulder to shoulder, celebrating in the streets as though it were Mardi Gras. The evening of the Final Four game, as we sat in our cold living room and watched Kansas squeak past Ohio State in the final seconds to go to the National Championship, our heads full of the explosive revelry that we knew was taking place in Lawrence right that very moment, I turned to Jim and said, "I want to go home." He looked at me for a few seconds, gauging the seriousness of my statement.

"I do too," he said. And he meant it.

After spring break, J's therapist thought she should take a break from therapy. She was pleased with J's progress, but frustrated with J's tendency toward being a glass-half-full kind of kid. "I'm not really sure there's much more I can do for her," she said. "But you can always call me if you need to."

You mean there's not much more you can do for a child with atheist parents who're going to hell, I thought.

On the third visit to the Maryland orthopedist he told me that though the bone in my foot still wasn't completely healed, I could transition back to regular shoes. It was a small thing, but it felt like a huge victory. Shoes! Soon I would wear real shoes again! After 10 weeks in the stank boot and another four weeks wearing an orthopedic sandal, the skin on the bottom of my foot was smooth as a salamander's. Walking across carpet barefoot was a strange new sensation: like walking on cacti. For many weeks, my foot hurt too much to cram it into a closed shoe, so I spent the cold days of spring wearing slide-type sandals with socks. My experiment with closed shoes lasted exactly two days. For the previous 20 years, I'd carefully trimmed the edge of my big toenail on my right foot to prevent it from becoming ingrown. But now it hurt too much to wrench the foot around to attend to the nail. By the end of the second day wearing the closed shoe, my toenail was firmly embedded in the skin of my toe, which was now swollen, pulsing and pus-filled. This necessitated a trip to the urgent care clinic for pain killers, antibiotics and a referral to a podiatrist. The podiatrist deadened my toe with three injections, trimmed off the edge of the toenail and treated the nail bed to ensure that part of the nail would never grow back.

The three of us learned many things about ourselves when we moved to Maryland, but one thing I learned about myself surprised me: I pretty much don't give a shit about the Civil War. Now don't get me wrong. I am knee slappin', deity praisin', punch-myself-in-the-face thankful that the North won the war. But I don't understand this American obsession with rehashing the Civil War again and again with an unapologetic shrug of the shoulders, as if both sides were equal in their quests and it doesn't really matter which side won. Maryland rakes in a lot of tourist dollars playing up the Civil War angle, and I guess because of that, they have to tread lightly. You can't very well insult all of your deep Southern neighbors who come through to visit Antietam or Monocacy to pay homage to great, great, great grandfather Zebedee, and in the process, drop a few bucks.

But we're from Lawrence, where John Brown started his rampage against slavery, ending it in Harper's Ferry, Virginia, where he aimed to start a well-armed slave revolt by raiding a U.S. armory. In Lawrence, there's an overwhelming view that John Brown was a force for good, whereas in lesser-informed parts of the U.S. he's sometimes referred to as a terrorist. In our part of the country, there's no question about the moral significance of the outcome of the Civil War, a fact that was driven home when we visited Harper's Ferry one afternoon, because I was determined that we'd have a good time no matter how much longer we had in Maryland. I'd called our realtor to let her know we were putting the house back on the market. Jim called Chuck to ask him to please not sell our Kansas home, because eventually, we'd be buying it back. In the meantime, I'd arranged several day trips as well as a trip to the beach in Ocean City. It just seemed to make sense to try to take advantage of our life on the East Coast while we were still there.

One Saturday afternoon, we visited Harpers Ferry, West Virginia, a charming, funky little town dripping with Civil War-era history. We just *had* to visit the grisly little John Brown wax museum, though Jim and I were regretting it by the end. The museum itself is sort of rinky-dink in a wonderfully weird way, but the bizarre wax figures and liberal use of fake blood freaked out J.

Jim chatted with a National Park Ranger whose interest was piqued when he learned that we'd recently moved from Lawrence.

"How do the people of Lawrence view John Brown?" he asked.

"We think of him as a hero," Jim said.

The ranger nodded. "Around here, people are pretty much in the middle when it comes to John Brown."

Our realtor seemed excited about selling the house she'd sold to us just four months prior. Jim and I discussed the madness of what we were doing. "What do I tell my boss?" he asked.

"You don't tell him anything," I said. "We put the house up for sale and see what happens."

"And what if it sells?"

"You sit down with your boss, tell him we're moving back to Kansas and see if he'll let you keep your job. If not …" I shrugged.

That was the big question.

It was about twenty weeks after breaking my foot that I felt comfortable enough to put on my trusty sneakers, the shoes in which I'd walked Rocky many miles. The sudden cease of his walks had been upsetting to him, and I imagined he wondered what horrible act he had committed to have been dealt such a terrible punishment. Walking was a slow, wonky process for me, and it would take more than a year to retain my natural gait, but I pimp-walked the dog around our new neighborhood, taking note of the disproportionate number of anti-dog-poop signs in yards and steering Rocky away from them. Our walks were significantly shorter than before, but Rocky didn't complain. He was thrilled to be out in the world again.

In the space of 40 days while our new house was on the market, there were 20 walk-throughs. We got used to packing Rocky up in the car and driving to a local park to kill time during the showings. As with most things in Maryland, it was a pain in the ass having to take Rocky with us because in our town, dogs weren't allowed in parks, even on leashes. So Jim and I would take turns walking Rocky around the perimeter of the park while the other one would play with J in the park proper.

After the house had been on the market about 60 days, we got the call from Addie we'd been waiting for.

"We have an offer on your house! And it's a good one!"

The buyers wanted into the house as soon as possible. In fact, they wanted in a week before school was out, something to which we couldn't agree. As I ended the call with Addie I realized that we would be leaving Maryland before we could take our trip to Ocean City. The hotel we'd booked refused to refund us the price of the room, a loss of about eight hundred dollars.

Though we'd discounted the house five thousand dollars from the price we'd paid just four months before, being a down market, the buyers figured they were doing us a favor and thought that we should pay the closing costs. Again. And because we were so desperate to get the hell out of Maryland, we asked if they might *please* pay a quarter of the closing costs, to which they agreed.

Jim made the call to his boss he'd been dreading, telling him that we'd sold our house and were moving back to Kansas. "I'd really love it if you'd let me keep my job," he said, "but I understand if you need to let me go." His boss said it would be fine, that Jim could work remotely and maybe fly out to visit the office quarterly.

We started repacking the half of our stuff that we'd unpacked.

Three weeks out from moving back to Kansas we received a three-hundred dollar invoice from the volunteer fire department for attending the wreck we'd been in. We could've been assholes and left town without paying the bill—which I suggested—but Jim went ahead and wrote a check, because that's the kind of guy he is. The firemen had been kind, and again, because of the dynamics of being located out in the county, their salaries were paid through donations and bills of service rather than taxes, so he figured it was only fair. Still, a little part of me wanted to take that bill, knock on the door of the family of the teenage girl who'd hit us and shove it down the throat of whoever answered the door.

Two weeks out from moving back to Kansas, the routine home inspections found that our Maryland house had termites. And radon. We hadn't had the house tested for radon when we moved in because we'd assumed the couple who'd lived there before us and had raised their family there would've done that. The termites hadn't been there five months prior. It cost about sixteen hundred dollars to mediate both.

One week before moving back to Kansas I received a phone call from the man who had come out from the moving company to provide our moving estimate and contract. I thought he was a timid sort of man when I met him, but I swear I could hear him sweating over the phone. "I've been working for this company for 15 years and I've never had to make a phone call like this," he said. "My boss says we're not going to move you. If I were you, I'd get on the phone to my boss right now."

"And say what?" I asked. My head throbbed. I wondered how I could possibly relay this news to Jim.

"If I were you, I'd call him right now," he repeated. "And keep calling until you get results."

I called. I got the boss' answering machine and left that sort of message that only a woman scorned can leave. I reminded the bastard that we had, in our possession, a signed contract. Then I phoned Jim and he raised his own hell with the moving company.

They agreed to move us, but told us that our possessions would be delayed a few days because their national affiliate had reneged on supplying them with a cross-country semi. Our things would be loaded, unloaded and placed in storage until a cross-country truck became available.

A couple of days before we'd pull away from our Maryland house forever, J summed it up best:

"It's like we've been eating bad luck."

The morning of our departure from Maryland we stopped at the realtor's office to sign the papers of the sale of the house and hand over the keys. Since I was wearing shoes again, I could drive my own car. Because we knew we wouldn't have our things for who knew how long, we packed our little Toyotas as full as we could with clothing, toiletries, laptops, pillows and blankets, and the air mattresses for sleeping. J rode with Jim while I transported the animals, who had the back seat, draped with a comforter, to themselves. We started out peacefully enough, and I hoped that since Max the cat had made this trip just five months ago, he'd understand what he was in for. But a couple of hours into the trip a foul odor emanated from the back seat. For an entire hour I told myself that it was extreme cat gas, because cats are so known for farting. Eventually, I couldn't deny the fact that the cat had shat in the car. We pulled off the highway where I bundled up the cat mess in the comforter and threw it in a dumpster behind a gas station.

After two days of driving, we were back in the old Kansas house, with its small windows and cramped kitchen. We collapsed on the ratty carpet with sighs of relief. It was beautiful. We had expected to walk in to a completely empty house, but were surprised to find that Nancy and David and their kids had filled our fridge with sandwich makings and fruit, leaving disposable utensils, plates and cups on the counters, along with a welcome home card. They even set up a folding table and chairs in the kitchen so we could eat up off the floor. For two weeks we camped in our old house, living out of our suitcases, sleeping on air mattresses, waiting for Maryland to get its shit together and get our stuff to us. We ate dinner out every night, hitting all of our favorite restaurants.

We loved every second of it.

It was the middle of June and roaringly hot. Daytime temperatures soared to 106, 107, 109 degrees. In the evenings, when it had cooled to a refreshing 99, we'd sit out on our back patio, soaking up the Kansas sunsets while the heat radiated from the ground. We'd swear we felt breezes that weren't there, as we listened to the sweet, hypnotic drone of the cicadas. Cicadas! One evening, it hit me. *That* was the sound that had been missing in the air in Maryland. The buzzing,

153

whirring, churning of billions of insects singing their sweet songs of sex, making the very air seem alive.

In just five months in Maryland we'd managed to visit seven doctors, total a car and completely drain our savings account. We also learned many lessons. We learned that despite our national stereotypes, there are snobs and rednecks peppered all over the U.S. In the end, we decided that the East Coast is a great place to visit, but not someplace we wanted to live. In the end, we decided that there's no place like home.

Four and a half months later, hurricane Sandy devastated Ocean City, Maryland. The town we'd briefly called home was too far from the coast to feel the serious wrath of the storm, but J's former grade school was closed for two days because the wind and rain was so intense. It's an irony that's never lost on me when I talk to people from the east or west coasts who are phobic of tornadoes: hurricanes and earth quakes often wreak far more havoc on far larger areas than do tornadoes.

A few weeks after we'd been back, my mother asked if it had been difficult in Maryland, and I replied that yes, it had been.

"Well," she said. "This whole ordeal has certainly been hard on *me*."

J's Worry Diary

J's therapist in Maryland suggested I keep a worry diary one week in between sessions just so she could read for herself what J was worrying about. Following is the diary I kept.

Thursday 2.15
Driving home from her first therapy appointment, J informs us that she's touched the bottom of her shoe and is concerned about touching her food that we picked up for her. We tell her that she can wait until she gets home to wash her hands before eating but she makes us promise that it's not dangerous to eat after touching her shoe and decides to eat anyway.

Starts an art project after dinner and asks us several times if combinations of glue, paper towels, water, salt and marker are poisonous in any combination when mixed together. We reassure her each time that none of these things are poisonous and she takes it pretty well. (We also remind her that she's worked with all these things for years and was never concerned about poison until recently.) Very happy while doing her art project. Washes her hands several times. (J LOVES doing art/science projects and always uses a wide variety of supplies when doing so.)

Before we fall asleep that night, she tells me she's worried about evil ghosts in the house. We talk about our new town, that we're both still a little nervous about the move but that there are things we're really starting to like here. She says she likes talking about that, that it makes her feel better. She falls asleep quickly.

Friday 2.16
Before she takes her shower for the morning, voices concern that she thinks her nightgown sleeve touched the toilet seat. We reassure her she's okay. Decides to do a little touch-up work on her art project before school. Asks me if Tacky Glue is poisonous. I assure her it's not. She washes her hands three times before school. She seems pretty happy until just before time to leave for school. Then becomes very concerned that her backpack has been on the school's floor, which might mean it's contaminated with germs/dirt/cleaning solution. She gets herself pretty worked up and upset just before leaving … J mailed a letter for me right before she and her dad left for school and her dad said that she was very concerned about the rust on the mailbox. Right before school and right before bed when she's tired seem to be big triggers.

J had several general worries over the afternoon and evening but didn't seem to really take anything too seriously and also seemed very content. ("Is this glue poisonous?" "No." "Okay.") But right at bed time as she was getting tired she bumped her head on the headboard of our bed while we were watching television and was concerned that she'd cracked her skull. I reassured her several times that she was fine and she went to sleep okay.

Friday 2.17
Lots of worries today and tonight. Didn't even bother to keep track of them all. Asked several times what would happen if rust got in one's eyes or mouth, even though it she'd touched the mailbox yesterday. Lots of other worries too. I remember once her being worried that she'd knocked a chip off her glass and could swallow it. She seemed happy, though, and said she'd had a good day at school. Worries got way worse right before bed.

Saturday 2.18
We drove to Antietam to look at the battlefield and monuments. J got out of the car several times to take photos but asked several times if anything on the grass or sidewalks was poisonous. We reassured her many times. Bought some stuff from the gift shop for her and she asked several times if any of the items could possibly be poisonous. We did start to become irritated with her because she's asking the same poison question sometimes five or six times. She didn't ever become too upset or take the worries too seriously today, though.

Sunday 2.19
Lots of general worries today. Lots of questions. We did become irritated with her a few times. I sat down to play with her in her room for awhile and that was fun. She seemed quite relaxed and it was a nice day. Right before bed J became very worried that she'd torn the membrane under her tongue and that it might be bleeding, or that she'd moved her eyes too far to one side and the muscles around her eyes might be bleeding. She asked several times if she could "bleed out." Reassured her

several times that she couldn't possibly bleed out and that she wasn't bleeding at all.

Monday 2.20
LOTS of worries today, I think because she has school tomorrow. Asking several times if things are poisonous. Concerned about stickers, the flowers we got for Valentine's Day and several other things. Has washed her hands several times. She seems pretty down today. Doesn't want to go to school tomorrow.

Amber Fraley is a writer, journalist, mother, L/G/B/T supporting pinko commie liberal living in the greatest city in America: Lawrence, Kansas. She blogs (upsets people) at http://dorothyofkansas.blogspot.com and can be followed on Twitter @Amberbobamber.

CPSIA information can be obtained
at www.ICGtesting.com
Printed in the USA
FFOW01n1804260614
·6085FF